Faustina

Faustina

Apostle of Divine Mercy

Catherine M. Odell

Our Sunday Visitor Publishing Division
Our Sunday Visitor, Inc.
Huntington, Indiana 46750

ISBN: 0-87973-923-1
LCCCN: 98-65847

Cover design by Rebecca Heaston

Printed in the United States of America

923

Contents

Blessed Sister Mary Faustina Kowalska of the Congregation of Sisters of Our Lady of Mercy (1905-1938). The portrait was taken in Plock in 1929.

Preface

Blessed Faustina Kowalska was a humble Polish nun who became the instrument for an extraordinary work of God in the twentieth century. Hers is a poignant and moving story, a brief life lived for the most part in obscurity, a life marked by great suffering and profound exultation, the life of a nun whose significance was largely hidden from her contemporaries. In this splendid book, Catherine Odell tells how Blessed Faustina Kowalska, God's humble servant, became the great apostle of Divine Mercy — the bearer of a message of grace and love to this most violent of centuries.

The life of Blessed Faustina, which unfolds in this book, calls for a response, a personal response from each of us. For guidance in this, we should look to how Pope John Paul II has responded to the message of Divine Mercy.

The Holy Father has taken a keen interest in Sister Faustina. As Archbishop of Cracow, John Paul II introduced Sister Faustina's cause for beatification; then in St. Peter's Square in 1993, he beatified her on the Second Sunday of Easter, known as Divine Mercy Sunday. The message of Divine Mercy has been a central theme of his pontificate. Mercy was the topic of his second encyclical "Rich in Mercy" (*Dives in Misericordia*) in 1981. Ten years later, on April 10, 1991, the Pope spoke about Sister Faustina at a general audience. He showed great respect for her, related her to his encyclical, and emphasized her role in bringing the message of mercy to the world:

> The words of the encyclical on Divine Mercy (*Dives in Misericordia*) are particularly close to us. They recall the figure of the Servant of God Sister Faustina Kowalska. This simple woman religious particularly brought the Easter message of the merciful Christ closer to Poland and the whole world. . . .
>
> And today? . . . Is it perhaps not necessary to translate into the language of today's generations the words of the Gospel, "Blessed are the merciful, for they shall obtain mercy" (Mt 5:7).

In 1997, John Paul went as a pilgrim to the tomb of Blessed Faustina. In a sweeping summary of the Divine Mercy message and devotion, he challenged us to be apostles of Divine Mercy like Blessed Faustina.

He begins by quoting Psalm 89: "I will sing of the mercies of the Lord forever" — a psalm he quoted at other significant moments of his life: at Fatima in May of 1982 in thanksgiving for his life spared, on his seventy-fifth birthday, and on his fiftieth anniversary as a priest. He proclaims the urgency of mercy: "There is nothing man needs more than Divine Mercy" — a message that is easily understood by those who "look upon the image of the merciful Jesus, His Heart radiating grace. Whoever sincerely says, 'Jesus, I trust in You' will find comfort in all his fears." The pope quotes his own encyclical "Rich in Mercy" (*Dives in Misericordia*): "The Church has the right and duty to appeal to the God of mercy 'with loud cries. . . .' I have come precisely to commend the concerns of the Church and of humanity to the merciful Christ. . . . I come to entrust to Him once more my Petrine ministry — 'Jesus, I trust in You!' "

John Paul II continues, "The message of Divine Mercy has always been near and dear to me. . . . In a sense it forms the image of this pontificate." He gives thanks for the grace of the institution of the Feast of Divine Mercy and for the beatification of Blessed Faustina. He recommends praying the Chaplet of Divine Mercy: "I pray unceasingly that God will have 'mercy on us and on the whole world.' "

How should we respond? Listen to the pope's challenge to the Sisters of Our Lady of Mercy in their extraordinary vocation as apostles of Divine Mercy: "I ask of you: accept this responsibility! The people of today need your proclamation of mercy: they need your works of mercy and they need your prayer to obtain mercy. Do not neglect any of these dimensions of the apostolate."

This is a challenge to all of us. We can all become apostles of mercy by being merciful in deed, word, and prayer as Blessed Faustina and John Paul II implore us to be.

Finally, I can respond to the exhortation of the Holy Father in his closing remarks: "*May the Divine Mercy transform people's hearts!* . . . We all need Divine Mercy so much as the third millennium approaches."

Read the life of Blessed Faustina with a heart open to the message of Divine Mercy. Read it prayerfully. Ask the Lord to show you how to respond to the challenge of John Paul II to let Divine Mercy transform your heart and be an apostle of Divine Mercy like Blessed Faustina.

Reverend George W. Kosicki, C.S.B.
Assistant Director, Divine Mercy International

Introduction

"There is nothing that man needs more than Divine Mercy," Pope John Paul II told the world at the grave of Poland's Blessed Faustina Kowalska in a suburb of Cracow on June 7, 1997.

The pope had come to honor the nun he beatified in 1993, and whom Jesus had named as His "Apostle of Divine Mercy" to this troubled, bloody century. It was certainly not the first time that Karol Wojtyla had visited the convent where the largely unlettered Sister of Our Lady of Mercy died an agonizing death from tuberculosis at age thirty-three in 1938.

After he was named archbishop of Cracow in 1964, he opened the investigation of Sister Faustina's life and virtues. But he had first heard about her during World War II. He was then a young seminarian studying in a clandestine seminary in Cracow. Poland was in agony, occupied by Nazi Germany.

Sister Faustina, gifted with the charism of prophecy along with many other gifts, had predicted Poland's war-time crucifixion. Responding to the promptings and visions given secretly to her, she also recorded the "Chaplet of Divine Mercy" and the "Novena of Divine Mercy."

Under the guidance of her confessor, Father Michael Sopocko, she directed the painting of the Image of Divine Mercy — Jesus with pale and red rays flowing from His chest, sending graces out to the world. And finally, the slender sister saw to it that a Feast of Divine Mercy was begun to commemorate Christ 's redemptive love — and mercy — on the Sunday after Easter.

Immediately after her death, Poland was in need of the Divine Mercy message and devotion. "In those difficult years, it was a particular support and an inexhaustible source of hope, not only for the people of Cracow but for the entire nation," Pope John Paul II admitted in June 1997. Poles stuffed the Divine Mercy prayers and pictures of Jesus into their pockets as they fled from their country, even when on their way to refugee camps. The devotions also spread very quickly to the United States. Father Joseph Jarzebowski, a Marian priest blacklisted by the Nazi SS, promised God that if he was able to escape from Poland and join members of his community in the United States, he would spread the Divine Mercy message. In May 1941 he arrived in Washington, D.C. With the help of Felician Sisters, a Polish order, he quickly began to print and distribute the Divine Mercy prayers and devotions, as did Father Sopocko in Poland.

From those roots, a flourishing and dynamic international Divine Mercy movement has sprung. The prayers have been translated into dozens of languages. There are Divine Mercy centers all over the world. Divine Mercy Sunday is celebrated as an official feast in Poland. And in 1996, more than ten thousand pilgrims attended a Divine Mercy Sunday celebration at the National Shrine of the Divine Mercy on Eden Hill, Stockbridge, Massachusetts. The shrine and international distribution center for Divine Mercy materials is administered from Eden Hill by the Marians of the Immaculate Conception.

And the diary of Blessed Faustina — four hundred seventy-seven pages of neat, tight script — has been translated and distributed throughout the world. It has since become a sort of handbook for the growing Divine Mercy movement. Sister Faustina began to write the diary in her Vilnius convent cell in the summer of 1934. Jesus and her confessor, Father Michael Sopocko, had ordered her to do it.

Having completed barely three semesters of schooling as a child in Poland, writing anything — except a few letters home — was an intimidating prospect. Nonetheless, Sister Faustina obediently complied and found a scratchy pen and a student theme book in a convent cupboard. Like the saints Catherine of Siena, Teresa of Ávila, and — most of all — Thérèse of Lisieux, who had been canonized in 1925, the year Sister Faustina entered the convent, this Polish sister inadvertently created a spiritual classic.

The diary of Sister Faustina is rich in mystical allusions and solid theological truths. It details the awesome journey of a soul striving to be and do whatever God wanted. Despite the austere religious conditions of her convent life and the traditions of a Polish spirituality unfamiliar to many of us today, her story speaks out.

The themes of persistence in the face of adversity, "active submission," fundamental trust in the Lord, faithfulness to the end, discernment, an ability to change the things that were changeable and the ability to be at peace with the unchangeable. Her diary presents all these things and more. It is a letter from one soul to another. And it is an account of her discovery of God's love. In the first notebook of her diary, she inscribed a title: *Divine Mercy in My Soul.*

Many years after the diary was written, Polish Cardinal Andrew Deskur, a theologian and a close friend of Pope John Paul II, wrote an introduction to the diary's official Polish edition. The work, he said, "is Catholic mysticism of exceptional worth . . . for the whole Church."

During her lifetime in half a dozen convents across Poland, this pretty young nun with freckles and gray-green eyes could not have been identified as a mystic capable of articulating dogmas and beautiful theological ideas. She was the convent gardener. She worked in the kitchen, the bakery, and the laundry. And yet, in recent years, the Congregation acknowledged her as its spiritual co-founder. She deepened her order's spirituality, showing new ways to fulfill its charism of cooperating with Divine Mercy to help rescue lost souls.

Her real mission, of course, had nothing to do with stirring soup or folding laundry — though she learned to do these, as the Little Flower of Lisieux had done them — in the spirit of absolute obedience and generosity for Jesus. Her real mission was hidden from almost everyone around her. It had to do with announcing God's mercy to a world increasingly steeped in sin and selfishness. "It is My will," Jesus told her, "that you should write. You do not live for yourself, but for others' souls. Write so that they might learn to love Me. Write of My mercy."

By the middle of 1936, the superiors of Sister Faustina's order understood that she was dying. A vicious and painful case of multiple tuberculosis was choking the young life out of her. Sister Faustina had known all along that she would not live long. In fact, she knew — and predicted — the exact date of her death. It was October 5, 1938.

During her final sickbed struggle in Cracow in 1937 and '38, Sister Faustina united her pain and suffering with those of Jesus, scourged and crucified. She prayed in particular for the dying, for priests and religious, and for her beloved homeland, Poland. She relived the torments of Christ's last hours many times, and she experienced the Lord's stigmata, though it was never visible.

Who could have predicted that a simple country girl would flower so exquisitely? Born to a poor, devout carpenter and his illiterate wife, Sister Faustina Kowalska (named Helena by her parents) was the third child in a family that eventually had eight mouths to feed. Her siblings loved her deeply, but they never imitated her astounding generosity, obedience, and piety.

Perhaps by the end of their own lives, her brothers and sisters understood more about the "Apostle of Divine Mercy" — their own Helena — whom Jesus had given to the troubled twentieth century. At the end of 1997, her eighty-two-year-old brother Mecislaus was still living near the family homestead in Glogowiec. He was the last of the Kowalski children alive. His older sister Natalia had died at age eighty-eight on January 24, 1997, after having spent her last months with the Sisters of Our Lady of Mercy at their convent in Biala, near Plock. It was at Plock that Sister Faustina first saw the image of the Divine Mercy of Jesus.

"I feel certain that my mission will not come to an end upon my death, but will begin," she wrote with her scratchy pen late one night at her desk upstairs in Vilnius. Her earthly end, in so many ways, was really a beginning.

Acknowledgments

Two splendid biographies of Sister Faustina gave to this author wonderful information and many insights into her life. The author is very grateful to Sister Sophia Michalenko, C.M.G.T., the author of *Mercy My Mission*, which was published in 1987. A special "thank you" also goes to Maria Tarnowska, the author of *Sister Faustina Kowalska: Her Life and Mission*. Her book was published first in 1989. Both authors sketched inspiring portraits of Faustina, the slender, frail lay sister whom Jesus chose as His "Apostle of Divine Mercy."

My personal thanks is also given to Father George Kosicki, C.S.B., assistant director of Divine Mercy International, for his gracious help. I'm also grateful for the wonderful materials produced by Father Seraphim Michalenko, M.I.C, vice-postulator of the canonization cause of Blessed Faustina, and for the encouragement received from David Came, Margaret Davey, and others at the Association of Marian Helpers at Eden Hill, Stockbridge, Massachusetts.

Many thanks to the Association of Marian Helpers for permission to use the photographs in this book. For further information on the Divine Mercy image, call or write the Association of Marian Helpers, Stockbridge, Massachusetts 01263; 1-800-462-7426. They are publishers of books, pamphlets, videos, audiocassettes, and related spiritual material about the Divine Mercy message and devotion.

And of course, this biography is most indebted to the rich, profound, and wonderful diary of Sister Faustina. The first Polish edition of the diary appeared in 1979, and an English translation was published in 1987 by the Marians of the Immaculate Conception at Stockbridge, Massachusetts. Anyone reading this biography, or any other about Blessed Faustina Kowalska, needs to understand this point: You will not truly "meet" Blessed Faustina unless you also read her diary. To read it is to journey day by day with an animated, gifted, and profoundly holy young woman who lived each day with the motto: *"Jezu, Ufam Tobie"* — "Jesus, I trust in You."

In this book, the Polish gender spellings of certain surnames have been respected. For instance, the masculine spelling is used in referring to a male or to a family, i.e. the Kowals*ki* family. But the feminine spelling — ending the surname with an "a" instead of an "i" — is used in referring to individual women, i.e. Sister Faustina Kowals*ka*.

Stanislaus Kowalski, Helena's father.

Marianna Kowalska, Helena's mother.

A Child Brimming With Joy

I experienced the definite call of God, the grace of a vocation to the religious life — **Diary, 7.**

Right after dawn, on August 26, 1905, thirty-seven-year-old Stanislaus Kowalski let his wooden cottage door slam behind him. Fingering his large black mustache thoughtfully, he headed quickly to the barn. Nations could rise and fall. Wars and revolutions might come and go. And babies might be born in the middle of the night, squalling insistently for attention, warmth, a mother's breast — and love. But — as Stanislaus knew so well — a farmer's cows had to be taken care of regardless of outside events.

Each day, the Kowalskis' cows were let out to graze on the five acres of sandy pasture that he owned near the village of Glogowiec. Later, when the animals were as satisfied as they could be with late-summer grass, they'd have to be brought back to be milked.

In the barn's dim light, the cows knew his step and swung their huge heads toward the opening door. Stanislaus was still humming the "Godzinki," the "Little Hours of the Immaculate Conception." He sang it aloud each morning right after rising to praise the Virgin Mary and God. He believed that a person should pray before anything else as each new day began.

This pious habit was certainly not this farmer's invention. It was common for Polish peasants to kneel inside or outside of the hut to pray right after rising. But Stanislaus Kowalski knew very well that he'd been especially blessed the day before.

His third child — and third daughter — had been born the previous night — on August 25. And thanks be to God, this birth had been an easy one. Their first two children, Josephine and Genevieve, had been born only after agonizing and terrifying labor for poor Marianna. But soon after this new child had entered the world, Marianna had smiled at Stanislaus with relief. Then the two of them had gazed quietly at the beautiful, tiny child they'd created. The Kowalskis had decided to call this third daughter (the future Sister Faustina) "Helena."

Stanislaus and Marianna Kowalski were country people living in the district of Lodz, in the very center of present-day Poland. The nearest large city, Lodz, was an industrial center which had begun to expand after textile mills were built there in the early nineteenth century. But Stanislaus was not drawn to city life. He was a country lad born May 6, 1868, in the village of Swinice in central Poland, not far from Lodz. Marianna was from the nearby village of Mniewie. Seven years younger than her husband, Marianna Babel was born on March 8, 1875.

Life near a Polish village was pretty quiet, and the young couple knew exactly what to expect when they joined their lives together on October 28, 1892, at Mniewie. Then they moved two miles down the road to the little farm near Glogowiec that Stanislaus already owned. A carpenter by trade, the young man reasoned that he would work his trade by day and tend to his farm the rest of the time. Like most Polish farmers, he tried to plant grains — usually rye, wheat, and sometimes millet. Potatoes were the staple of a Polish family's diet, but some form of grain was also served along with the potatoes at every meal.

Stanislaus had reasoned that even a little profit from a good crop would take the edge off raw need. And years earlier, he'd bought the cows. Pro-

The Kowalski home in the village of Glogowiec, the parish of Swinice Warckie, where little Helena was born and spent her childhood.

ductive milk cows were necessary for a man who hoped to raise a family. Like most Polish cooks, Marianna didn't use much milk in her cooking except perhaps for a few holiday dishes; it was too precious. But now, their children needed milk.

Everything had been in place at the stone and brick roadside cottage when the newlyweds arrived at their little farm late in the summer of 1892. A new life did begin for both of them, of course. Marriage asks for adjustments from both husband and wife, but Marianna's life undoubtedly changed more than her husband's. Stanislaus was very strong-willed. His vision of the way things should be was fairly rigid. But Stanislaus was also older than Marianna. He had already met the world head-on as a carpenter — a man with a needed skill for sale.

In the mind of young Kowalski, the patriarchal authority he held over his home and wife was God-given. At the same time, Stanislaus did not spare himself for his family's welfare or for the honor of God. He worked hard during every waking moment. And there was a good reason why he belted out hymns and prayers when he rose from his bed in the morning.

Praising God, giving thanks to God. It was a man's — in fact, anyone's — duty. And Marianna agreed — although she might have seen no reason why her pious mate couldn't praise the Lord in a whisper, or even in his heart.

In the first nine years of their marriage, Marianna Kowalska had whispered many prayers herself. She had begged God for the blessing of children. Her mother too had prayed for this intention. Finally, those prayers were being answered and the Kowalski cottage was now filled with the laughter and cries of children. Stanislaus and Marianna were elated to see their family growing. And this newborn, tiny Helena, born in the thirteenth year of their marriage, seemed like such a special little joy.

Stanislaus switched the cows and coaxed them down the road to better pasture. "Hey, hey, get going, girls," he called to them. He reminded himself that he would have to walk two miles to Swinice later in the day to see the pastor of St. Casimir parish, Father Joseph Chodynski. The proud father had to arrange for little Helena's baptism on the following day. The child's godparents were already chosen. They were Marcin Lugowski and Maria Szewczyk Szczepaniak.

After little Helena's baptism, the days of autumn and harvests came quickly for the Kowalskis. Two-year-old Genevieve and four-year-old Josephine hovered over their new baby sister, waiting for her to grow big enough to hold. By Christmas, the infant — like most three-month-olds — could coo, smile, and wave her little arms and legs excitedly. She was paying more attention to the sights and sounds around her while her parents spent their energies keeping their little cottage warm. For the winter at least, the world of tiny Helena was contained within the four walls of a simple country cottage.

But on those evenings when the Kowalskis were singing Christmas carols to their three tiny girls, a stocky, white-haired man in white was pacing up and down in his rooms in Rome, about seven hundred miles away. Pope Pius X would have been comfortable in the home of Stanislaus and Marianna Kowalski. Born into a poor Italian family, Giuseppe Sarto wished that the same rich faith he would have seen in the Kowalskis could be found in the rest of Europe. But this was not so.

In other countries — especially in France — there was a deep and dangerous hostility toward the Church and her rightful influence over the lives of people. It was the situation in France which was bringing great grief and sleepless nights to the seventy-year-old pontiff. On December 11, 1905, France had passed a law of separation which took control of church properties away from the dioceses and parishes. The year before, religious teaching had been banned in French schools. Religious orders were outlawed and priests, sisters, and brothers were forced into exile. Freemasons had gained power in the French government and were dedicated to the eradication of Church life.

During the last days of December, the pontiff formulated his plan. He decided to fight the French government with the only "weapon" at his disposal. On February 11, 1906, he issued an encyclical, *Vehementer Nos*. This letter stated that the Laws of Separation violated divinely established authority and were unworthy of France. A second encyclical, issued in August of 1906, defended the Church in France in even stronger terms. Pope Pius also consecrated fourteen new bishops and sent them back to France. He was not about to let faith wither and die there.

If the Polish Catholics heard or read about the battles their pope was fighting with France, they would have undoubtedly approved. The Poles were very familiar with struggles for freedom. As Helena Kowalska was learning to crawl and then walk during the summer of 1906, the people of her land longed for the day when they could stand and move again as an independent nation. In 1906, there really was no Poland on the map of Europe.

In 1772, the country had lost a third of its territories to its neighbors — Austria, Prussia, and Russia. In 1793, Russia and Prussia had robbed Poland of even more territory. Lithuania and the Ukraine, on Poland's eastern side, were added on to Russia. And on the west, Prussia took most of western Poland. In 1795, the three neighboring nations simply carved up what was left of the Polish middle. As a nation, Poland disappeared.

The Poles revolted in 1863, five years before the birth of Stanislaus Kowalski in Swinice. Russia had begun to draft Polish men into its army and the Poles couldn't take this latest insult to their national identity. But Russia cracked down viciously on the rebels. The Russian language was made the official language of the regions near Lodz and to the east of Kowalski's native village. In 1871, Prussia formed the German Empire. Poles under Prussian rule in the west were forced to adopt the German language.

By the twentieth century, men like Stanislaus Kowalski had hidden their political feelings and dreams. And hopes for Poland were kept quietly alive inside the cottages. All official documents — including baby Helena's birth certificate — were written in Russian, in the conqueror's language. And while the Poles prayed for the rebirth of their nation, the people were sustained by a tenacious religious faith. That fed their spirits, just as the coarse rye bread and potatoes sustained their bodies.

Despite the imposed Russian language, little Helena heard only Polish in the Kowalski home. Her first short prayers were Polish. Very soon, she was no longer the baby of the family, as other children were born to Stanislaus and Marianna.

A fourth daughter, Kazimiera, was born in 1907, but died as a baby. Then, in 1908, Natalia was born, and Bronislawa followed soon after that. But this new baby also died in infancy. In 1912, the first boy was born, and Stanislaus and Marianna proudly named him Stanislaus (Stanley) after his father. A second boy, Mecislaus, blessed the family in 1915. Marianna Lucyna (or Mary) was born in 1916, and Wanda, the last child, was born in 1920.

Even as a very little girl, there was something deep, something very spiritual in Helena, or "Helenka" (little Helen). Stanislaus and Marianna noticed it right away. Helena listened attentively when her father read to the children from the Bible, from books about the saints and missionaries. And this third child, a pretty little girl with straight features, gray-green eyes, and auburn hair, prayed her prayers for long periods of time.

One morning when she was five, Helena joyfully awoke and told her family about a wonderful dream she'd had. Mary, the Mother of God, had held her hand and strolled with her through a beautiful garden. Like most very young children for whom there is no separation between the conscious and unconscious, Helena probably saw the dream as a real experience.

Most children are contemplatives by nature. But the Kowalskis knew almost nothing about contemplative prayer and the fact that God calls some to a more intensive life of prayer. Apparently, they found Helena's religiosity strange and confusing. And it was indeed different from the behavior of their other children. Before she was seven, Helena often woke and sat up in bed in the middle of the night. Those pretty eyes were wide open, and the little girl would kneel and begin to pray. Marianna wasn't completely comfortable with her daughter's late night vigils, but Helena calmly told her, "My guardian angel must be waking me to pray." By the age of five or six, therefore, this little girl understood that God and supernatural realities were just as real as the sturdy wooden table on which her mother prepared the family's meals. Likely as not, her father had made that table.

When she was seven, however, something new took place. One evening, at Vespers, during the Exposition of the Blessed Sacrament at the parish church, Helena "heard" Jesus in a new way. He spoke to her soul, and the little girl, who was already attuned to spiritual communication, heard what the Lord had to say. Her heart must have been racing madly.

"I experienced the definite call of God, the grace of a vocation to the religious life," Helena recalled in matter-of-fact fashion in her diary, many years later. The child apparently understood that this was "an invitation to a more perfect life." She must have had so many questions about what it would be like to live this "more perfect life." Where would she live? Could she see her big sisters, Josephine and Genevieve, often? How old would she be when this new life began? Would she live alone or with others? She knew almost nothing about the religious life, and had few answers to these questions, until she entered a convent many years later.

But Helena didn't trouble her busy mother or father with her concerns. Perhaps she sensed that they didn't know how to answer her. And maybe something told her that Jesus would guide her when the time was right.

However, Helena had changed in some way. From that evening in 1912 or '13, she knew that her future would be different from those of other little girls in the neighborhood. They giggled together. And with few toys, they may have made summer necklaces from the sweet clover her father's cows had overlooked. Helena Kowalska knew why her future would be so unique. With hands pressed tight against her young face, she had quickly whispered "Yes" to that early invitation from Jesus Christ. At the tender age of seven, she really did intend to live a "a more perfect life" — whatever that meant.

Helena knew, of course, that she was to be obedient to her parents and help them as much as she could. She worked very hard at this, trying perhaps to please God as she pleased an extremely strict father. She shielded her brothers and sisters from her father's switch when a punishment was coming their way. And neighbors often remarked that it didn't seem as though Helena truly belonged to a family which had so many ornery children. "She was different," everyone said.

Helena was creative in her efforts to help out. One time, she decided to surprise her father. She got up very early to take the cows out to pasture on a Sunday morning. Cows had to be cared for seven days a week. Helena hated to miss attending Mass on Sunday. So she had been an early bird in order to get the job done. Singing the "Godzinki" at the top of her voice, she was leading the three cows back on one rope as she met her astonished father.

"To tend to one cow would have been difficult enough, but to manage three on one rope!" her father later exclaimed. He'd been prepared to take his belt to her until he saw that she'd kept the animals out of his rye fields.

Occasionally, Helena would also set up a "store" to sell little homemade dolls and trinkets to other children. Nothing cost more than a *zloty* (penny) or two. Helena recruited help for this project and the children from the area loved it. When the store closed, however, Helena gave away her proceeds to help the "poor" children.

Over the years, Helena had become a favorite child of both of her parents. She was pretty, even-tempered, and extraordinarily helpful and obedient. Marianna and Stanislaus already knew that they'd always want Helena close to them. She was too precious to ever give up. Helena had been helping with household tasks for some time. She also took care of the younger children and often read to or entertained them. She was a good little mother and a good teacher as well. When it was her turn to take the cows to pasture, Helena had a retinue of children trailing her. When she'd led the cows far enough, she would settle the little ones comfortably in the tall, meadow grass.

Almost always, Helena told her little groups dramatic stories from the Bible or from books about saints and missionaries. These stories fed her religious imagination. But she made the stories wonderfully exciting for the children too. She talked about the virtues that God's special friends bravely tried to live by. Even children should try to live virtuously, she explained. Helena often said that she wanted to be a hermit or missionary some day. She admitted that she was anxious to eat roots, drink only water, and work for God. A bunch of youngsters shook their heads in amazement, but were ready to join her.

Helena's older sisters and even the younger Kowalski children saw that this sister was different. She never fought the patriarchal authority with which her father Stanislaus ruled the family. He ruled life at home with an iron hand, and Marianna was not often able to restrain it. One time, he severely punished little Stanley for breaking off some twigs from a neighbor's willow tree. It wasn't as if the boy had damaged a fruit tree, but his father was furious.

The other Kowalski children, longing for more time to play, would try to weasel their way out of chores. Not Helena. In fact, she often tried to persuade them to be obedient, cooperative, and even docile. Helena was not trying to be better than anyone else. She simply saw life differently — even at the age of nine.

A loving God had created all and established authority on earth. That authority helped to guide people back to Him. Parents were given authority in families. Even if their parents had unfair expectations of them, it must be part of God's plan.

But there was something in Helena that made Stanislaus and Marianna uncomfortable. They didn't really understand their daughter's intense attraction to deeper prayer. They tried to put some normal boundaries on her spiritual enthusiasm. Helena conformed, but not for long.

After the summer of 1914, the Kowalskis — and most other Polish families — needed every zloty they could find. World War I began with the assassination of the Austrian Archduke in Sarajevo, about four hundred miles from Lodz. Germany and Russia declared war against each other and against many other nations on August 1. Poland became a primary battle ground.

The Kowalski children likely heard their father chatting quietly about the war with neighbors. Russian officials made their rounds in the region, and it wasn't a good idea to talk openly about politics. What would this war mean for them, the farmers wondered. At forty-six, Stanislaus was not concerned about being drafted by the Russian Army. But he and his friends probably tried to see what might be in store for Poland. Could their nation be born again? Could it survive in this twentieth century?

Near the end of the summer of 1914, the seventy-nine-year-old pontiff, Pope Pius X, died in Rome. He was saddened by the horrifying future he foresaw for Europe. He knew that the war wouldn't solve the great tensions that existed between many nations and ethnic groups. Pius had tried to promote unity and peace during his papacy. Believing that the Eucharist was the sacrament of unity, he had called for more frequent reception of Holy Communion. And in 1910, he urged that children be prepared for the Eucharist at earlier ages.

Sometime in 1914 after her birthday in August, nine-year-old Helena Kowalska was very busy preparing for her First Communion. She had learned to read, and was reviewing her lessons several days each week with the pastor, Father Pawlowski. War talk was in the air around Swinice. But

Helena was filled only with joyful anticipation. The mystery of Jesus hidden in the Blessed Sacrament had fascinated her since her earliest days. Bursting with an intimacy that she already felt with Jesus, she tried several times to prolong the family's evening prayers. "*Nie* [No]," Helena," her parents told her firmly.

On the morning of her First Communion Day, Helena got up, got dressed, and rushed to her parents. She kissed their hands and begged their forgiveness. It was an old Polish custom of respect and contrition for an offense against a parent. Perhaps Father Pawlowski had reminded the girl of the tradition. Neither Josephine nor Genevieve had done it before her. A few weeks later, Helena made the custom a weekly ritual. She would beg forgiveness from her parents before she went off to confession.

On the way home from her First Communion, several neighbor women stopped her. Helena was walking home by herself. And, indeed, she seemed to be in her own world, overflowing with joy.

"Why aren't you going back with the other children?" one of the women asked the green-eyed little girl.

"I'm going with Jesus," replied the beaming Helena. Seeing one of her fellow communicants, she couldn't contain herself.

"Are you happy about today?" Helena said, stopping the girl.

"Yes, of course," her friend said. "Look what a pretty dress I'm wearing."

The girl with no pretty dress whispered with a smile, "I am happy because Jesus has come to me." There was no artificiality in her response. She was completely happy and completely convinced that Jesus was within her.

It was good that Helena's First Communion came during 1914. Even before Christmas, Stanislaus could see that the new year would probably bring great suffering. The "landlords" of Poland — Austria, Russia, and Germany — were at war with each other. Some Poles were pro-Russian; some were pro-German. Everyone was hearing promises of Poland's freedom and independence when the war was over. It was hard to believe such promises. But it was tempting.

In the meantime, there was little chance for a man like Stanislaus Kowalski to sell the extra grain that he might harvest on his little farm. Travel was severely limited because of the war. And soon, there were famines. Marianna managed to cook with the few vegetables they raised, but there was no money for anything extra.

Helena, who was almost ten, was grieved that there was no money to buy proper clothes for church. Because the three older girls had only one dress among them, they had to take turns attending Mass at St. Casimir's.

Despite the need in their own household, Helena felt a deep compassion, a connection with those who had even less money than her own family.

"When Helena was about ten years old," her sister Josephine remembered, "she decided to obtain money for the poor in the same way that they do. She dressed in rags and went around the village from house to house saying a prayer and asking for alms. She came back home very depressed saying, 'The poor have a terrible life. How much they have to bear getting food for themselves.'"

It was a remarkably intuitive observation for a ten-year-old girl, growing up in a tiny Polish village. Helena Kowalska could see that the poor needed to be treated with mercy, generosity, and love. Perhaps some of the villagers had nothing to spare. But Helena, whose family had almost nothing to give away, would have understood that. There must have been some rude responses, some doors slammed in her face, to explain the depression Josephine noted in her younger sister. What a sad lesson to learn! A child, brimming with good will, saw how much some people must suffer when others deny them fundamental mercy and respect.

2

Finding Her Way to God

*It was in the seventh year of my life that, for the first time, I heard God's voice in my soul; that is, an invitation to a more perfect life. But I was not always obedient to the call of grace. I came across no one who would have explained these things to me — **Diary, 7**.*

"*Prosimy, dzieci* [Come in, children]," Helena called, standing inside the Kowalski doorway.

Like her older sisters, Josephine and Genevieve, Helena was a protective little mother when Marianna Kowalska was out or busy. She would also "mother" and nurse the pets and farm animals when they were sick or injured. A dog's cut leg might need some disinfectant and a bandage. A feeble chick might need more protection than the rest of the hen's brood. Helena's heart was always touched by their needs.

Ten-year-old Helena also may have been told to keep her younger siblings indoors during the autumn and winter of 1915. The war was moving much too close to the little farms and villages of the region. In fact, the front lines drew very near Lodz. There was terrible tension in the air. No one really knew what would happen to their families and to the widespread hope for a new Poland.

At the beginning of the summer of 1915, German submarines had sunk the English passenger-liner *Lusitania* near Ireland. More than a thousand people had died. If the farm families around Glogowiec hadn't heard about that tragedy, they'd heard plenty of other terrifying news about the war.

The Kowalskis had their own battles to fight. They were virtually destitute. There never had been any savings. And with the war raging not far away, Stanislaus was limited in the income he could make at carpentry. The wealth of the Kowalskis was in their tiny patch of Polish land and in their faith. Stanislaus and Marianna prayed very hard at St. Casimir's when they were able to attend Mass. They prayed for peace. They prayed that God would help them keep their children warm and fed during the coming winter.

Helena prayed too. She probably knew little about the international tensions and jealousies which had kindled the war. But she was a perceptive and sensitive child. She knew that war was killing people and destroying families all over Europe.

Times were very hard. The Kowalski girls took turns going to Sunday Mass because they had to share the one good dress the family owned. On the Sundays when she had to stay home, Helena would find a prayerbook and retreat to a quiet corner. During the Mass time and after, she would read the prayers and then meditate. Helena could find her own temporary cloister in the middle of the busy Kowalski cottage. And she let nothing disturb her period of prayer. Often, her mother would call her to come and help her, forgetting what time it was. But on these occasions, Marianna's third daughter ignored her mother. Later, the girl would apologize. "Don't be angry, Mother," Helena pleaded. "I had to fulfill my duty towards God."

There were also family duties, of course, and they were numerous. Most of the chores Helena shared with fourteen-year-old Josephine and twelve-year-old Genevieve. Typically, these three older Kowalski children would have spent much of their day in school. But the Russians had closed the

St. Casimir Church, Swinice Warckie, where little Helena was baptized, made her first confession and Communion, and received her first calling to the consecrated life.

schools in their Polish territories. Children had to learn what they could at home. Stanislaus taught his children to read.

Helena loved to read some of the mission magazines and the biographies of saints which her father had collected and stored on their small bookshelf. More than the other Kowalski children, she was attracted to stories about men and women who lived lives of exceptional holiness. Helena would sit at night, imagining what it was like to kiss a leper, as did the brave Francis of Assisi. In the dull orange glow thrown by one of the family's oil lamps, she pored over the accounts of Francis Xavier, Elizabeth of Hungary, Anthony the Hermit, and Agnes, the early Christian martyr.

In addition to taking care of the younger children and the livestock, Helena spent time sweeping the floor, cutting up vegetables for soup, mending clothes, mixing and baking bread. It had been difficult to feed a big family even before the war. Marianna taught her daughters to be as inventive and resourceful as possible. But maybe all Polish cooks were exceptionally creative in this respect. Some bread bakers put a large cabbage leaf underneath the big round loaf of rye before it went into the oven. The cabbage leaf moistened the loaf and kept the bread from sticking to the pan. It was a neat Polish cook's trick and made use of what was available.

Helena saw that her mother used whatever she could find to feed the family. But there was so little money, so little food. And yet, in the midst of great suffering, the Kowalskis and thousands of other Polish families felt some hope for a better future. The flame of Polish independence was a tiny candle flickering in the breeze. No one knew if the light would be extinguished with the next sudden puff of wind. On the other hand, more and more Poles were coming to believe that their nation's freedom could burn brighter and brighter.

By 1915, the Polish patriot Jozef Pilsudski had made an alliance with Austria. He led Polish forces in driving all Russian forces out of Poland. But with the Russians ousted, Germany and Austria — war allies — tried to absorb the Polish territories that Russia had held. In 1917, Roman Dmowski formed the Polish National Committee in Paris. This committee worked to win support for an independent Poland. And in the following year, after the Allies had won the war, an independent Polish republic was born. Jozef Pilsudski was the first chief of state.

In 1917, life was already normalizing for the Poles. With the invading armies driven out, there was a new hope, a frenetic energy spreading. For the first time in her life, twelve-year-old Helena Kowalska was enrolled in the Regional District School at Swinice. As she had already been reading for several years, school officials placed Helena in the second grade.

Helena was very happy to finally go to school. She had a good mind and loved to learn. She was unfailingly respectful and attentive to her teachers. For years, she had delighted others with her gift for story-telling and her animated way of bringing Scripture lessons alive. Now, as a student, Helena learned quickly.

One day, the school inspector arrived at Swinice to visit the recently reopened schools. It was important to make sure that the children who had been denied schooling for so long were finally given a good education. After the children were introduced, the inspector watched as a pretty, slender, dark-haired girl stood up. Clearly, she was prepared, though her dress for this formal occasion was simple and patched. It was Helena Kowalska. In a loud, clear voice, she recited the poem "The Father's Return" ("*Powrot Taty*") by the Polish national poet Adam Mickiewicz.

> Go, children, all together,
> Out of town, to the post on the hill
> Kneel there at the miraculous picture,
> Piously say your prayers. . . .

The poem was about a merchant whose wife — the narrator — urges her children to pray at an outdoor shrine for their father's safe return. Later, when the father returned, he was attacked by robbers who released him, having overheard the children's prayers.

Helena's gift for bringing animation and emotion to the ballad was apparent. The school principal beamed with pride when Helena was later awarded a prize for her fine recitation.

Helena Kowalska's happiness as a student didn't last. She attended school only three terms when, in the spring of 1919, she was asked to leave. There was no problem with her personally. In fact, her teachers and the school's principal undoubtedly regretted the situation. But space in Polish schools was painfully limited. Helena could read and had at least fundamental skills in writing and math. Room had to be created for younger children.

And so, in the autumn of 1919, fourteen-year-old Helena was at home full-time again. She had reached the age when young girls are typically preoccupied with the way they look, with what their friends think of them, and with what life will bring. But Helena's adolescence was different. She had her share of normal adolescent concerns because she was quickly becoming a woman.

But Helena's spiritual life set her apart from her older sisters and from most young girls. In fact, now that school was no longer a part of her life, she began to be drawn more and more into prayer. She longed to communicate with God, to feel God's presence. Each night, Helena's prayer vigils would begin when the little Kowalski cottage was finally quiet.

At fourteen, Helena was seeing strange, bright lights during her prayer. These lights must have been confusing to her, because she mentioned them to her parents. Fifty-one-year-old Stanislaus and Marianna, now forty-four, didn't know what to make of such a report. They had no understanding of mystical experiences and their connection with their daughter's profound prayer life. They told her quite emphatically to quit imagining such things. Apparently, Helena did not try to talk about her spiritual life with anyone else — not even with the parish priest at Swinice.

This rebuff by her parents made Helena feel quite lonely. She really had no one with whom she could discuss the way she felt, the intense and growing attraction to God. God was a magnet of incomparable strength. This teenager was being pulled so close to Him that she knew that her life would have to change somehow.

Helena's interior life, the life of her spirit, was an undeniable reality to her. And yet, it was hidden from everyone around her. Her sisters, brothers, and parents lived in a different reality — one marked to a much greater degree by the mundane necessities of farming, keeping house, and feeding a family.

Sweeping the dusty floor, hanging up the laundry, cooking the vegetable soup. All of these things Helena did. But, more and more, they were becoming superficial, detached from the life she longed to lead. Without knowing much at all about the religious life, Helena felt that she would have to live life differently. She wanted to serve God exclusively with her life and with her work. She just didn't know how it was to be accomplished.

In the meantime, Helena was surprisingly patient. She tried to live a life that was perfectly pleasing to God. She especially tried to please and accommodate her parents — even when the expectations of her mother and father were unreasonable.

One evening when she was fourteen, Helena was asked to accompany her eighteen-year-old sister Josephine to a party in Swinice. It was after midnight when the girls returned home with one of the young men at the party. Helena's uncle saw his nieces and the young man and apparently told Stanislaus that some of the behavior he witnessed wasn't totally proper. The uncle may have been exaggerating or imagining improprieties. But the enraged and humiliated father lashed out at both girls before he asked any questions. The girls tried to explain and hid behind the chairs, begging their father to listen. But it was useless.

Helena accepted the rebukes and the whipping with great grace. In fact, she even accepted some responsibility for the shame her father felt over his daughters. "For this sadness I caused him," she told herself, "I must make up a hundredfold by bringing him honor, not shame."

During the spring and summer of 1920, Helena committed herself to growing in virtue in her own small village of Swinice. Halfway across Europe, in a tiny village in France, French families were rejoicing. On May 16, Pope Benedict XV canonized their own Joan of Arc, who'd been born in Domremy in 1412. More than four hundred fifty years after her execution by burning at Rheims, this unschooled teenager was recognized for her heroic virtues and was named a saint. As a very young girl, Joan had decided to listen to God's voice and direction, no matter what happened.

If young Helena had heard or read about St. Joan, the newest saint of the Church, she was bound to be inspired. Helena still loved to hear about dramatic deeds of virtue and courage done for God. And Joan's life was rich with such deeds. She had given everything to do God's will as she saw it.

Helena still didn't know how to follow God with the total commitment of a Joan of Arc. But she knew that some changes in her life would be helpful. In the spring of 1921, fifteen-year-old Helena approached her mother about working outside the home. Helena still had no proper dress to wear to Church. The income that Stanislaus brought in as a carpenter and farmer paid only for bare necessities. She wanted to make a little money.

Marianna looked at her third daughter, who was so different in personality from her first two girls. But Josephine and Genevieve were already working as housemaids and earning a bit of extra income for themselves. It was good for them. And no doubt about it! With Helena also out of the house, there would be one less mouth to feed!

"All right, you can go to work," agreed Marianna, smiling as she saw Helena's face lighting up with happiness. Helena was still a favorite in the house, and it wouldn't be easy to let her go. And Stanislaus would also miss her terribly. Marianna knew that. But, perhaps this pretty, green-eyed daughter of theirs would find her place in the world. And she wouldn't be too far away.

And so, a few months later, sixteen-year-old Helena went to live and work as a maid in the town of Aleksandrow, near Lodz. Helena knew the family. They owned a bakery, and Mrs. Helen Goryszewska was the sister of the Kowalskis' neighbor. Helena received her room and board, and of course, a small salary. In return, the young girl did the cleaning, some cooking, and took care of the family's little boy. She agreed to work for the Goryszewskis for one year.

Mrs. Goryszewska quickly grew very fond of this competent, respectful young lady. Helena was amazingly efficient at everything she did, and her employers particularly liked the way the teenager entertained their little son. He eagerly sat on Helena's lap and listened as the pretty girl with auburn hair told him stories. And Helena must have been happy to earn a little money to take care of her own needs.

Helena's employers noticed some unique traits about the girl they'd hired. After all, she lived with them. Mrs. Goryszewska noticed that Helena was very pious and devout. What she probably did not see was that Helena was often praying silently as she worked and that she could not sleep at night because of the strange bright lights she'd reported to her parents years earlier.

And one day, the light blazed during the daylight. The experience jolted her.

Helena was walking out of the Goryszewskis' house to the courtyard. Perhaps she had some laundry to wash or to hang up. Maybe she had to fetch some vegetables or herbs to prepare the family's supper.

As Helena glanced up, she gasped and covered her face with her hands. "*Ogien! Ogien!* [Fire! Fire!]" she shrieked. It looked as though the whole courtyard was in flames. Instinctively, she backed up toward the door and continued to warn the household about the fire.

Inside, Helen Goryszewska panicked when she heard the girl screaming. Perhaps one of the bakery ovens had overheated, she thought to herself. Picking up her little boy to take him with her, she ran to the courtyard to see for herself. Just as she arrived, she saw her frightened young maid faint and collapse. There was no fire anywhere! And yet the girl's expression had been one of sheer terror. When Mrs. Goryszewska's husband came running up to her — his hands dusty with flour — she explained what had happened.

"Better send someone for the doctor," the wife whispered to her husband. "And send for someone from her family." This young girl had to be going crazy! She'd apparently been petrified by a fire which didn't exist! The baker nodded his head in agreement.

Later in the day, a local doctor told the Goryszewskis that he'd found nothing wrong with young Helena Kowalska. But Josephine, Helena's oldest sister, arrived soon after that to see what had happened. She'd been sent by her parents. They were understandably concerned. Helena reluctantly confessed to Josephine that she'd seen a light again. But she added, "Tell Mommy not to worry. I am not crazy, but I shan't say anything more about it to them. I shall not be staying here long."

For Helena, there was no longer any real mystery about these phenomena. She knew that the beautiful brightness she saw in her dark room was a beacon. She was to follow the light and come closer to God. Finally, during the early months of 1922, Helena could wait no more. She told Mrs.

Goryszewska that she would not be able to work for her any longer. And, despite some prodding from the older woman, she was evasive about the reasons she was quitting. At home, Helena's mother and father were surprised to see her.

"I want to enter a convent," Helena calmly and directly told her parents.

The moment had come. Helena was going on seventeen. From the age of seven, she'd known that she was called in a special way by God. Waiting for an answer, she glanced at her father's weathered face and the long, dark, heavy mustache which jutted off his checks below his mouth. Her mother's expression was one of agony mixed with fear. Tears were silently welling up in those tired eyes.

For many years, Marianna had seen this conflict coming. She and Stanislaus did not want their favorite child leaving their tight-knit, God-fearing family for a mysterious existence in a convent. Helena would be too far from their cottage door. The girl's parents understood that religious life was a worthy calling, a holy vocation. But they knew almost nothing about what that life would mean for their daughter. During the Russian occupation of their region of Poland, the convents had been confiscated and the sisters scattered. There were no convents near Glogowiec; the people had very little knowledge of religious life. Into that vacuum of ignorance, some unspoken suspicions and fear had settled.

And in her heart of hearts, Marianna knew something else. She and Stanislaus were getting old. Someday, someone would have to care for them. They wanted that someone to be Helena, their sweetest, most selfless child. Swallowing hard, Marianna stared at her lap where her hands fidgeted nervously with the folds of her skirt.

Helena saw that her father was biting his lip. He was thinking about what she had said. The girl waited — praying and silently begging him to agree.

"*Nie, Helenka*," he said finally, slapping his knee emphatically and standing up. "*Nie!*" He said it again, looking straight at his daughter's stricken face. "This is not the life for one of us. We cannot afford the dowry that any convent would want. They all ask this dowry because when you enter religious life as a nun, you become a bride of Christ. I give what I can to the Church, but a dowry I cannot give! It is out of the question. Forget it!" Stanislaus Kowalski then left the house and headed quickly for the barn. As far as he was concerned, the matter was closed.

Inside the house, Helena saw that her mother's face was no longer full of fear. Marianna's expression had softened, showing a sense of relief. Helena now knew that her mother didn't want her entering the convent any more than her father did. But Marianna at least tried to comfort her shattered seventeen-year-old. Tears of grief streamed down the young face. And Helena now knew that no one in this house would help her to reach her dream. In the happy Kowalski home, there was a new and tragic sense of discord, a quiet uneasiness.

"I first learned from Helenka of her desire to enter the convent after she returned home from Aleksandrow," Josephine remembered later. "We were all very shocked by this, because at that time, people knew very little about the religious life. Our parents were very sad, and the children were crying."

Motherhouse of the Congregation of Sisters of Our Lady of Mercy at 3/9 Zytnia Street in Warsaw. Helena entered religious life here, but the building was later destroyed in World War II.

3

Vision in a Dance Hall

"Go at once to Warsaw; you will enter a convent there" —
Words of Jesus to Helena, **Diary, 10**.

During the autumn of 1922, seventeen-year-old Helena Kowalska felt strangely isolated and abandoned. In the cottage where she'd been born in Glogowiec, she was lost. She was no longer comfortable in the only home she'd ever known. She knew that God wanted her somewhere else.

"Daddy, I don't need any money. Jesus Himself will lead me to a convent," Helena had told her father when he said that she couldn't enter religious life. But Stanislaus wouldn't listen to such childish prattle. Money was not hanging from trees for well-intentioned teenaged girls. Helena knew that her father's decision was the final word. She brooded, and performed her old chores mechanically.

Finally, Helena talked to her mother about finding another job. She still needed money even if she wasn't going to the convent. Marianna could hardly object. The child was right. Arrangements were soon made for Helena to live in Lodz with relatives, the Rapacki family. The Rapacki home was her base until Helena located a job with three women who were members of the Third Order of St. Francis. Members of Third Order communities are lay people committed to the spirituality and some of the ministry of their order. They live in the world and don't take vows of poverty, chastity, and obedience.

Helena's new job didn't pay too well, but she didn't seem to care. Her schedule permitted her to go to Mass each day and also to visit the sick and dying people in the neighborhood. Something in her held on to the dream of religious life. She fasted to add sacrifice to her prayers. In fact, when her father's cousin, Michael Rapacki, teased her about her goal, she was quick to respond. "I will go and serve God because that is what I resolved to do since my childhood," she told him.

In fact, however, the girl's resolve was weakened by her parents' point of view. She became discouraged and gave in to hopelessness. There were so many obstacles! For some months, she pushed the promptings of her call to the back of her mind. She began to buy attractive clothes, including a lovely rose dress. She began to go to a few dances with friends. She was almost "too elegant" when she applied for a new job as a maid at the home of Mrs. Marcianna Sadowska in Lodz.

"Helena came to me so fashionably dressed that I hesitated to hire her as a maid," Mrs. Sadowska recalled years later. Mrs. Sadowska may have presumed that the girl would not want to work too hard. And so, she offered her a salary that was lower than the amount she'd intended to offer. But Helena didn't argue and accepted it.

On the morning of February 2, 1923, Helena knocked at the door at 29 Abramowski Street. She was starting her third job and was to work as a maid and babysitter for the three Sadowski children. While Marcianna worked in her grocery story, Helena handled things in the home.

Helena's employer couldn't have been happier with her. Helena seemed to anticipate the jobs Marcianna wanted done. And the girl's pious practices were impressive, almost shocking for Marcianna Sadowska, who didn't really practice her faith. Every Wednesday, Friday, and Saturday, Helena abstained from meat. During Lent, she ate no meat at all and abstained from milk products on those three special days of penance.

One day, Josephine Jasinska, Helena's older sister, came by to visit and Mrs. Sadowska sent Helena to the store for a treat. When Helena came back with a honey bun, Marcianna asked, "Helen, why didn't you get some meat?" "Not today, Mrs. Sadowska," Helena replied. "It's a fast day."

More than this commendable religiosity, however, this working mother loved the way that Helena would gather the three Sadowski children around her for stories in the evening. The children loved Helena, while she delighted in them. Helena enchanted them or had them laughing hilariously within minutes. She never tired of her role as a loving "big sister."

But Helena was eventually as restless in this job as she was in the positions she'd held earlier. Without explaining her reasons, Helena told Mrs. Sadowska that she would be leaving her post. Because her employer was expecting another baby, Helena stayed on longer than she wished to stay. She left employment with the Sadowskis on July 1, 1924, after their new baby was born.

Emotionally, Helena was tired of living with ambiguity about her future. In her heart, she knew that God was calling her. But it was impossible for her to answer that call! Her parents would not permit her to enter the convent. This inner turmoil was exhausting. Something had to give. She herself says that, for a time, she slipped into a more worldly lifestyle. One night, she went to a dance with her sister Natalia at Wenecja Park in Lodz. The music was lively and everyone seemed to be having a good time. Even Helena was hiding her feelings well. But in her soul, she later wrote, she was experiencing "deep torments."

"As I began to dance, I suddenly saw Jesus at my side, Jesus racked with pain, stripped of His clothing, all covered with wounds." Jesus then spoke to Helena and said, "How long shall I put up with you and how long will you keep putting Me off?"

As soon as she saw this vision of the suffering Christ, Helena was in another world. She no longer heard the music or saw the young man she'd been dancing with. In this moment and in this place, there were only two individuals — Jesus and herself. But then, just as quickly as it began, the vision ended.

Helena, shaking and pale, took a seat near her sister, pretending to have developed a headache. After a while, she slipped out of the dance hall and made her way to the Cathedral of St. Stanislaus Kostka. Though there were a few people inside the church, the eighteen-year-old threw herself on the floor in front of the Blessed Sacrament. And in her heart, she begged the Lord to tell her what to do. Immediately, the Lord spoke to her: "Go at once to Warsaw; you will enter a convent there."

It was the confirmation that Helena Kowalska needed. She had wanted religious life. She had asked her parents to support her desire. But they didn't — or were afraid to. Though the desire to be a nun had never died within her, there had been many moments of doubt about how it could be accomplished.

Helena walked to the Rapackis's home, where she was living. She packed her things and went to bed. In the morning, she went to tell Josephine about her plans. When she returned to the house, she had big news for the cousin she called "Uncle Michael."

"I am going to Warsaw to enter a convent," she told him.

"My God, Helen!" he shouted. "What are you doing? You know that this will make your dear mother and father very sad and break their hearts!"

Suddenly, there was a lump in Helena's throat. He was right. Her parents would be grieved, but she knew that it was also the right thing to do. She gave "Uncle Michael" the nice clothes and things she had bought and asked him to give them to her family. Inside the bundle, there was something designated for each member of her family. The clothes, including her beautiful rose-colored dress, would look nice on her younger sisters at home. They had no money for such pretty things, and having some nice clothes would make them happy.

"And what will you have?" Michael said. He stared at the bundle she'd handed him. It was as though Helena was bequeathing things to her family in anticipation of her death. And then Michael glanced at the tiny bag in Helena's hand. That bag obviously held very little.

"What I am wearing is enough," Helena said, her voice full of confidence and conviction. "Jesus will take care of all my needs."

Nonetheless, when Helena sat down in the train later that day, she began to cry. "Mother will say I ran away from home when she finds out about this," she murmured as she pressed her tear-streaked face into her hands. She wept so pitifully, Michael later confessed that he would have taken her off the train if the engineer hadn't signaled it was about to pull out. As the train lurched forward and blew its shrill whistle, Helena headed toward Warsaw.

Poland's capital city was about one hundred thirty miles to the northeast of Lodz. Helena had never been far from home before. And as the train gained speed, Helena's head and eyes hurt from crying and she finally became quiet. The textile factories, churches, shops, and tiny houses of Lodz streamed past. The urban scene finally yielded to fields of rye, wheat, and sugar beets. That looked more like home to her, and the country girl from Swinice sensed that this train ride would be one of the most significant journeys of her life.

The rhythmic clackety-clack of the train was calming. When the train pulled into the Warsaw station late in the afternoon, Helena was jerked quickly back into reality. She stepped off the train into a crowd and into confusion. She knew no one in this huge city. There were beautiful parks filled with flowers, old palaces, and the tall spires of churches built in the Middle Ages.

But she had no desire to be a tourist on this warm summer day. She tightened her grip on her small bundle of belongings and prayed for guidance. "Mary, lead me, guide me," she prayed. It was getting dark and she had nowhere to stay.

Immediately, Helena received the answer in her heart. She was to get a ride out of the city to a nearby village to stay for the night. She did as she was directed, and returned to the city the next morning. Not knowing what her next step should be, Helena entered the first church she came across. It was St. James Church on Grojecka Street, in a Warsaw suburb. Helena went in and prayed for further guidance during the Masses being said there.

During one of the Masses, Helena again received the divine direction she desperately needed. "Go to that priest [Father James Dabrowski, pastor of St. James] and tell him everything," she was told. "He will tell you what to do next."

When Helena had explained her situation to Father Dabrowski, he directed her to the home of Mrs. Aldona Lipszyc, a solid woman of faith whom he knew well. Helena, he knew, would be welcome and safe at this home until she found a convent to enter.

Helena gratefully accepted the hospitality extended by Mrs. Lipszyc, whose husband knew Father Dabrowski well. There were four children in the family and the mother had been looking for a maid. It was another perfect arrangement for Helena. Helena earned her keep and still had time to investigate the convents in Warsaw. In her free time, she visited them, introduced herself, and explained her interest in becoming a sister.

Locating a convent was an intimidating task for young Helena. Mrs. Lipszyc advised her about which convents to visit and how to get to them. Making her way through the huge, sprawling city was difficult. The summer sun baked the old brick streets. It was strange not to feel the breeze or find some shade from trees in the open countryside.

But by now, Helena Kowalska's manner and even her appearance may not have made a good impression on the nuns she visited. She had given away her best clothing to her family. Though her employer supplied her with a suitable dress, Helena's self-assurance fell flat now and then. And that was not surprising.

Helena understood that she would probably need a dowry before she was accepted by any religious order. She didn't have one. But she persisted in her attempts anyway. Time after time, however, she was refused. It was obvious that she was poor, not well educated, and had training only for menial work.

"We do not accept maids here," many convents told her before closing their doors in her face. After a few weeks, the girl became discouraged. "Sorrow gripped my heart," Helena wrote in her diary years later, "And I said to the Lord Jesus, 'Help me; don't leave me alone.' "

One day, Helena walked up to the imposing brick motherhouse of the Sisters of Our Lady of Mercy. It stretched out, a block in length, at 3/9 Zytnia Street. Once again, she knocked. Her stomach was churning with the anxieties she felt. And yet, she held fast to a slender strand of hope.

"What do you want?" the Sister Portress asked Helena.

"I wish to enter the convent," Helena answered, using the words she'd used many times before.

When she was invited into the parlor, Helena sat and soon met the Mother Superior, Mother Michael Moraczewska. The Superior had been secretly observing the girl from the next room. She too noticed what all the other convents had noticed. Helena was penniless, poorly educated, and without valuable skills.

But Mother Michael had also noticed some nice qualities in the girl as well. The auburn-haired girl with freckles had a refreshing simplicity and sincerity about her. And Helena had an attractive and engaging manner. Sizing her up from the next room, the Superior had decided to give the girl a chance.

In the parlor a few moments later, Mother Michael talked briefly with Helena. Her first impressions were confirmed. The girl was likeable, attractive, and sincere, despite her lack of means. Mother Michael then told Helena to go to the Lord of the house and ask whether or not He would accept her. Helena understood that she was to go to the chapel and appeal to the Lord in prayer for an answer.

"Immediately, I heard this voice," Helena later wrote of this moment: "I do accept; you are in My Heart." With joy bubbling over in her young heart, Helena rushed back to the Superior, and told her of the Lord's response. "If the Lord has accepted, then I also will accept," Mother Michael told Helena with a smile.

Mother Michael then sat down again with Helena. They needed to talk. She didn't want to extinguish the beautiful joy that showed in the girl's face. But she explained that Helena would have to find the funds for a wardrobe, even if the convent graciously dispensed with the dowry requirement.

The two agreed that Helena would work to get the money and bring it periodically to the convent for safe-keeping. When sufficient money was made, Mother Michael told Helena, the Sisters of Mercy would accept Helena with open arms.

Helena stood up to leave, beaming with joy over the plan. Mother Michael noted again that the girl truly was lovely. There seemed to be something special about her, and at this happy moment, Helena was radiant. Mother Michael offered her blessing and said good-bye. Then, the portress showed the future postulant to the door.

It was finally done! Helena had found a home with the Sisters of Our Lady of Mercy. She could hardly believe it as she walked down Zytnia Street. She stopped right where she was to say a prayer of thanks. How good God was! And to think that she would be joining the Sisters of Mercy! It seemed right! Even perfect! Helena rushed back to Mrs. Lipszyc's house to tell her the wonderful news, singing the "Godzinki."

4

Helena Becomes Sister Mary Faustina

I had stepped into the life of Paradise. A single prayer was bursting forth from my heart, one of thanksgiving — **Diary, 17.**

"The Sisters of Our Lady of Mercy." "I'm joining the Sisters of Our Lady of Mercy." "I'll soon be entering the convent of the Sisters of Our Lady of Mercy!"

During the remaining summer days of 1924, Helena Kowalska surely reminded herself aloud that God's mercy would soon bring her to the Sisters of Mercy. In her mind, Helena often reviewed the many reasons she had to rejoice for the convent she would enter.

She had liked Mother Michael Moraczewska and the way the Superior had welcomed her. Mother Michael had made Helena feel at home. She had not belittled her for her poverty and minimal education. And she may have liked the Mercy Sisters' habit. It was simple and graceful, with a white neck-band collar and white cap beneath the black veil, which attractively framed the face.

And the idea of being a Sister of Our Lady of Mercy touched her profoundly. Helena believed that the Mother of God had been leading her to religious life for many years. When the girl had time to think about it all, tears of happiness welled up in her eyes. "For the Sisters of Our Lady of Mercy, thank you, God!" she whispered.

The congregation had been founded in Laval, France, in 1818 by Thérèse Rondeau, a wealthy young woman. She was touched by the plight of French girls pulled into prostitution by their poverty. Miss Rondeau founded the "House of Mercy" to take in, educate, and reform these fallen girls. After some hard times, a congregation formed and spread to serve this social need; there was great demand for it. The founder asked her sisters to treat the girls, or "wards," with utmost charity and mercy. In 1862, the Sisters of

Our Lady of Mercy had been established in Warsaw. They had built the huge convent at 3/9 Zytnia Street that young Helena Kowalska visited on a summer day in 1924.

In the fall and into Warsaw's hard winter, Helena's heart was at peace. She worked harder than ever, cleaning, cooking, and doing the laundry for the Lipszyc family. They noticed that she often sang hymns while she worked. But as far as Helena was concerned, babysitting for the Lipszyc children was never much like work.

She loved taking care of the four youngsters and loved being with them. She could enter their worlds, leaving behind the "grown-up" constraints. When the children wanted to play masquerade, she dressed up in costumes along with them. They were fascinated by her skill at making up games and telling stories. Whenever Helena was with the children, peals of laughter filled the house. She was full of fun and love. And as always, children loved her for it.

After the work day was done, Helena periodically added up the zlotys that Mrs. Lipszyc paid her. She estimated that she would have enough money to pay for her wardrobe in the summer of 1925. Then, she would make her way quickly to Zytnia Street.

While Helena was dreaming of making her home in a convent, her affable employer was imagining a different future for her. Mrs. Lipszyc was lining up suitors for the young woman. Perhaps Mrs. Lipszyc couldn't bear the thought that this vivacious and attractive girl would be "shut away" in religious life.

Helena understood that Aldona's intentions were good-hearted and even generous. Nonetheless, she discreetly but firmly discouraged the young men who were steered her way. She explained that she'd given her heart to God.

More disturbing was the pleading appeal that Helena received from her parents. They wanted her to abandon her plans to enter a convent and come home. After she wrote a letter about her plans, her parents had sent her sister, twenty-two-year old Genevieve, to visit her in Warsaw. Stanislaus and Marianna still did not understand or accept Helena's resolution to become a nun. They simply could not see things as she did.

© Marians of the Immaculate Conception

Mother Thérèse Rondeau, foundress of the Congregation of Sisters of Our Lady of Mercy in Laval, France.

Helena talked frankly with Genevieve about her goal and how much she wanted religious life. She admitted that the only thing delaying her acceptance by the Sisters was money. When she had enough money to pay for her wardrobe, she would be received as a postulant.

The two young women then chatted about the family news and what was going on in the village where they'd grown up. But Genevieve realized that "Helenka" — as their father called her — could not be persuaded to come home.

"Helenka" was the favorite child of Stanislaus and Marianna. And yet, she hadn't been spoiled at all by this status. Genevieve could see that her younger sister was quite mature and settled. These Kowalska girls — so close in age — had crossed the threshold into womanhood. But Genevieve and Helenka had very different goals in life. In a way, they hardly knew each other any more.

With a shared heaviness of heart, Genevieve and Helena parted in the morning. Genevieve left the Lipszyc house to return to Glogowiec. Helena said "good-bye" and turned her attention to her morning responsibilities as a maid. Each one knew that there would be great anguish in the cottage later in the day when Genevieve walked in — alone.

Helena herself felt very sad about the situation. She regretted that her parents had not accepted her call to a religious vocation. She knew that she could never go home because of the choice she was making. But she had also been wounded by her family's attitude. She was alone in her joy. No one who knew her well seemed to understand her desire for religious life. Nobody congratulated her on her plans, on the single-minded focus with which she now scrimped to save as much money as she could.

Sometime in the autumn, Helena took sixty zlotys to the Sisters of Our Lady of Mercy and gave it to them. It was a downpayment against her wardrobe fee. Through the winter and into the new year of 1925, she continued to save everything she could. She was investing her money and her heart in religious life. But she went about her duties in the Lipszyc household, smiling politely as Aldona mentioned the fine qualities of one young man after another.

As the first summer flowers began to bloom in Warsaw's gardens, Helena could see that she would soon be able to make the final payments for her habits and convent clothing. By her calculations, she could enter the convent near the end of July. Her longing to finally spend her life fully in God's service was growing stronger each day.

June 25 was the Feast of Corpus Christi, a great celebration of the love of Jesus in the Eucharist. It was a wonderful feast to Helena. Since her First

Communion at the age of nine, she had never stopped rejoicing in the Body and Blood of Jesus. During the octave following the feast, something new took place during an evening vesper service.

"I came to know how very much God loves me. Eternal is His love for me," Helena later wrote. This gift of new understanding about God's love flooded the girl's spirit. And, just as newlyweds are moved to profess their love for each other, Helena needed to respond to God's gift. In her heart, with simple words, she made a vow of perpetual chastity. She promised that her body, as well as her spirit, would be given to God alone. She vowed that she would never marry, never enjoy the sexual intimacy of married love, nor the happiness of having children.

Helena's vow of chastity came even before she entered the convent. In a sense, it was the final "investment" of her spirit in religious life. It took place when she was also making the final installments of money to the motherhouse. "From that moment," Helena later reported in her diary, "I set up a little cell in my heart where I always kept company with Jesus."

Early on the evening of August 1, Helena "floated" down Zytnia Street. She walked up to the huge wooden front-door and pulled the bell. When the door swung open, she was warmly welcomed. It was the day of her entrance into the order. It was the vigil of the Feast of Our Lady of the Angels, and Helena herself felt that she had "stepped into the life of Paradise. A single prayer was bursting forth from my heart, one of thanksgiving."

Helena was shown to her sleeping quarters and given the clothing she was to wear as a postulant. Postulancy, as in most religious orders of women, was the first stage of commitment in the Sisters of Our Lady of Mercy. The word postulant means "someone who requests." In a short postulancy period, candidates ask to be admitted to religious life as they learn what that life will mean. The second stage is called the novitiate, which usually lasts from one to two years.

Novices are truly members of their orders, but they are accepted in a limited and temporary way. They still have to complete the novitiate program, which forms and educates them in deeper ways. At the conclusion of the novitiate, the novices profess temporary vows of poverty, chastity, and obedience. Later, after several years of discernment, the religious man or woman has the chance to make a full commitment to the community by making permanent vows.

Helena was received as a co-adjutor in the order. Her new congregation included two groups of nuns. One group was called directresses. These women were well-educated and were teachers for the "wards" — the troubled women and girls that the congregation served. The nuns who were coadjutors, or members of the second choir, did the housework for the community and offered up their prayers and sacrifices for the success of the ministry.

Helena had known very little about the actual work of the order she joined. She was so happy to be accepted by any convent that she hadn't thought much about what she would actually do in the convent.

If the girl had been properly informed, she would have known that some religious orders are "contemplative," some are "active." In contemplative orders, the members basically devote themselves to prayer. In active orders, the religious men or women are primarily involved with active ministries, such as teaching, health care, social work. Without realizing it, she had asked to be admitted to an active congregation which ministered to troubled women and girls.

Soon after Helena entered the congregation, her former employer, Mrs. Lipscyz, visited the convent. She had been asked to give a character reference for Helena. Mrs. Lipscyz knew that the gregarious girl would be challenged by the structured, controlled life of a convent. Privately, she assured Helena that she could always come back to them if religious life didn't work out. Aldona was only nine years older than Helena. The two of them had had many open and warm conversations during the time Helen had lived with the family.

In Helena's postulancy class, the women spent three months under the guidance of Sister Margaret Gimbutt. She was an older, prayerful nun. She was very relaxed and intuitive as a directress of postulants. And that was very encouraging to Helena.

Nevertheless, the exhuberance Helena had felt on the evening of her entrance had fizzled within three weeks. In fact, by August 22, she was a bit depressed and distressed. She hadn't known what to expect of the convent. Now, she was told to walk slowly, to speak only when spoken to, to pray in chapel only at appointed times. This was enormous regimentation for a girl who'd been independent and had a lively spirit. And she believed that too much of her day was filled with housework!

Doing the laundry, washing dishes, cooking — Helena was very bothered by the routine. She had joined the convent to have more time to pray. In these first three weeks, her days in religious life were not so different from her days as a household maid!

Helena was still very young. She should have realized that caring for any household — even a convent household — would require plenty of labor. Some nuns would have to roll up their sleeves, plunge their arms into wash buckets, and scrub the floors. With hundreds of mouths to feed, other women would have to spend a great deal of time cooking. The wonderful and idealized vision Helena may have had of a nun's life was quickly destroyed.

Helena soon concluded that she'd made a mistake in her choice of a convent. She steeled herself to meet with the Superior. She planned to tell Mother that she wanted to transfer to another convent — a convent of "stricter observance." She had heard that in this type of convent, there might be more time to spend in front of the Blessed Sacrament, more time for prayer and contemplation. As it was, Helena was often being corrected by her superiors for "only wanting to pray all the time."

One August night, a frustrated Helena decided to talk to Mother Michael the next morning. Then Helena went to pray for guidance in the little chapel. She knew that she would need fortitude and patience in choosing a new religious order. The house was quiet as Helena knelt to pray. The other nuns were in bed. Despite her pleading for inspiration, Helena received none in the chapel.

With a heavy heart, she finally got up from her knees and returned to the dormitory. As she was getting into bed, separated from her sisters by curtains, she impulsively dropped to the floor to pray face-down once more. She didn't know that it was against the rules to pray in her cell after nine p.m.

Helena was desperate. She truly wanted to know God's will for her. It seemed clear that she should search out a convent where she could spend more time in prayer. And yet — she had no peace in her heart about making such a change.

She prayed, pleading for an answer. Her face was in her hands, pressed against the hard floor. Suddenly, she was aware of a light glowing brightly above her. As Helena raised her head from the floor, she saw the wounded face of Jesus upon the curtain that hung near her bed. There were cuts and gashes on His face. Tears flowed slowly down his face and dropped upon the bedspread of her bed.

"Jesus, who has hurt You so?" Helena whispered to the suffering Christ.

"It is you who will cause Me this pain if you leave this convent," the Lord told her. "It is to this place that I called you and nowhere else; and I have prepared many graces for you."

Helena begged pardon for her error, and the vision faded. With her heart at peace now, Helena remained on her knees praying for a while. She thanked God for showing His will to her. Her questions had been answered. She knew that she should remain with the Sisters of Mercy.

When she finally stood up and got into bed, she was exhausted. Helena could hear the steady, rhythmic breathing of several of her sisters sleeping nearby. It was a comforting sound. All of the sisters in this quiet house were members of her new family. And soon, Helena too was sleeping.

On August 25, Helena turned twenty, but she may not have thought much about this milestone. The emotional struggles had been very hard on her psyche in recent weeks, and she soon became ill. Her years of fasting had been unsupervised by a trained spiritual director, and Helena's young and sturdy body may have suffered. At this time, she was thin — too thin.

In fact, this collapse may have been the first ominous manifestation of tuberculosis. If so, it was hidden. And those around the young woman could only judge her state of health by what they saw. The Superior was shocked by the young woman's exhaustion. But no one on Zytnia Street had any hint of the psychological trauma she'd been through.

Helena, along with two other sisters, was sent to rest in a rented summer house in Skolimow. The young nun's only job was cooking and she enjoyed that. In the little house, there was more time to rest and talk with the Lord. It was wonderful. And one day, Helena asked Him what direction her prayer should take. She wondered if she should be praying for anyone in particular.

Again, there was a vision. This time, it was a vision of purgatory. And, as Helena described it many years later, she seemed to actually enter the vision, accompanied by her guardian angel.

In a "misty place full of fire," she wrote, there was a crowd of suffering souls. The souls were "praying fervently, but to no avail, for themselves." Helena realized that only the living could aid them with their prayers. Before she left, she asked them what their greatest torment was. The longing for God, they replied. However, the souls also added that the Mother of God often brought them refreshment.

As Helena and her angel left the fiery mist, she heard the voice of God explain, "My mercy does not want this, but justice demands it." From then on, Helena prayed frequently for the souls in purgatory. She had seen firsthand how desperately souls in purgatory longed for the soothing mercy of God. If her prayers would lessen their agonies, she was determined to embrace this ministry. Helena did it wholeheartedly. She did it, thanking God for putting her to good use.

Near the end of spring 1926, the group of postulants prepared for entrance into the novitiate by making an eight-day retreat. Helena and the others were to receive their habits and their religious names in the traditional clothing ceremony on April 30. Each postulant would process to the altar in a white wedding gown, symbolizing her marriage to Christ. Then, presented with her religious habits for the first time, she left the church only to return quickly, dressed in her religious habit.

Helena wrote to her parents to invite them to her clothing ceremony. But Stanislaus and Marianna did not come. In fact, no one from the Kowalski family was there. One of Helena's sisters later explained that her letter had arrived too late. Though disappointed, Helena still hoped that her parents would soften their views and accept her vocation. But on the day of her clothing, one more event confirmed that God had surely chosen her.

When Helena stood with the other postulants in front of the altar to receive her religious habit, she fainted. Later, as she was putting on the habit, she fainted again. Those around her assumed that the girl was nervous, keyed up. One of the nuns ran to get some smelling salts.

On this first day of her religious life, Helena was given another vision. And it was overwhelming. In a flash, God showed Helena just how much she would suffer for Him during her life in the convent. She "saw" the physical sufferings, the mental anguish, the periods in which she would be misunderstood or even persecuted. The vision of all that pain came to her in an instant.

The realization of what she was accepting in religious life shocked and frightened the twenty-year-old. And that was why she collapsed into the arms of older nuns, who later teased her for being faint-hearted. "But then God filled my soul again with great consolations," Helena recalled later.

The name that Helena Kowalska was given on this clothing day was "Sister Mary Faustina." The name was given to her by the Mother General. The name "Faustina" meant "the fortunate, happy, or blessed one." Helena's name may have been the feminine form of Faustinus, a martyr from the early Church whose feast was celebrated on February 15. According to legend, Faustinus and his brother Simplicius were thrown into the Tiber River in Rome for refusing to worship Roman gods near the year 120. Seven months later, their sister Beatrice was martyred for her faith as well.

But Helena added something else to this ancient name. She wanted to be known as "Sister Mary Faustina of the Most Blessed Sacrament."

Sister Mary Faustina must have been very happy walking down convent halls in her new habit. Giving her life for God was exactly what she'd wanted to do since childhood. And by now, the new sister understood that she was to be "martyred" on a daily basis. Extraordinary suffering was to be her lot in life, her special ministry. She was to intercede for God's mercy for others with every breath, with every work and prayer.

On the other hand, knowing about the pain, the agonies that were to come her way didn't fill her with dread. There was great joy on the pretty, fresh face of the new Sister Faustina. And she relished the name she'd been given. Martyrs like St. Faustinus had often been the heroes in stories she had told, as she sat with her back up against a tree in her father's pasture.

5

Into a Dark Night

*Going deeper into myself, I could find nothing but great
misery. I could also clearly see the great holiness of God. I did
not dare to raise my eyes to Him, but reduced myself to dust
under His feet and begged for mercy* — **Diary, 23**.

The two-year novitiate of Sister Mary Faustina began peacefully and joyfully — even after visions of her painful future made her faint during the
clothing ceremony.

The first year of the novitiate at the Sisters of Our Lady of Mercy was
called the canonical year. It was to be spent in deepening the sister's spiritual life and in educating her regarding the fundamentals of the faith and
the history of her congregation and its constitutions. The sister-in-training
also learned more about religious practices and the vows that she would
one day take.

In the early life of a nun, superiors are the primary teachers about religious life. They often have a very powerful effect on the postulants or novices who are entrusted to their care. A directress of postulants or novices
acts as a spiritual confidante and guide. She helps to steer the newcomer
towards a well-balanced and God-centered spirituality, and she trains her to
adapt to the special expectations of that religious order. As this stage of
Sister Faustina's religious life began, she tried to subdue some fears about
what was coming next.

In some ways, Faustina's first superior, sixty-seven-year-old Mother Jane
Bartkiewicz hadn't supported — or understood — her very well. The months
of postulancy in 1925 had been extremely hard on the young woman. As a
former Vicar General for the congregation, Mother Jane was an advocate
of unquestioning obedience. She believed that her postulants had to bend
to fit into religious life. If there were personality traits or characteristics
which made it more difficult to follow the convent rules, these traits needed
to be removed — much as one would scour a stain from the sink. The

gregarious Helena Kowalska had often felt the vigorous, determined scrubbing arm of Mother Jane. In fact, during those first few vulnerable months of convent life, Faustina had wondered if she could ever meet the standards of her directress. That had led to some depression.

Following Mother Jane's instruction, Faustina's class had moved to Cracow and was briefly directed by Mother Margaret Gimbutt. Mother Margaret had been as gentle as a dove with her young novices. She tried to form them by example. Faustina was grateful for Mother Margaret's wonderful style of leadership

But Sister Faustina didn't need to worry about Mother Mary Joseph Brzoza, who took over as directress of the new class of novices in Cracow on June 20, 1926. In her, the novices found a wonderful blend of qualities. With deep-set, expressive eyes and a warm smile, this thirty-seven-year-old nun was loving and motherly. But she was also firm, spiritually perceptive, and had great gifts of discernment. These gifts were soon very helpful to Sister Faustina, who still had plenty to learn.

During the summer of 1926, Helena had become used to her new name in this convent family. She was now "Sister Faustina." To prevent herself from tripping, she learned to catch a few folds of her long black skirt between her fingers when she was climbing the stairs or kneeling. And she gradually began to create the internal discipline she needed to respect "holy obedience."

In the convent, "holy obedience" regulated every action and word of the sister. Prayer in chapel was scheduled for a particular time. Recreation was slotted for a particular time. Meals, private prayer, work in the kitchen, Mass — everything in a sister's day had its appointed time and boundaries.

Though Sister Faustina failed many times to perfectly live by this challenging lifestyle, she soon saw the rationale for it all. Within this rather rigid framework for life, God could use individuals to guide one other to holiness. And so the young sister who'd left home at sixteen began to conform in her will and way of doing things.

The remaining months of 1926 went well for her. The twenty-one-year-old Sister Faustina had many reasons to believe that she was in the right place.

Faustina was very popular among the other novices. They jokingly dubbed her "the lawyer" because of the way she gestured while talking during recreation periods. As always, she was amiable, talkative, and ready to use her gifts as a wonderful story-teller. But both Faustina's peers and her superiors could see that there was a deep and profound love for God in her. "Jesus in the Eucharist was, to her, a living person with whom she wanted to talk at every free moment," observed Sister Crescentia Bogdanik.

Sister Crescentia was about the same age as Faustina, but she was a senior novice — older in religious life. Like every other senior novice, Crescentia had been assigned to act as an "angel guardian" for a junior novice. She was given Faustina as her charge and, for months, she observed Faustina closely, becoming increasingly impressed by what she saw.

There was a special kinship between the two, and the leader or teacher role which Crescentia held quickly disappeared. Faustina was just as elated with her new friend. For the first time, she had met someone who felt just as intensely as she did about the Lord. The two young women became friends for life.

One day in Warsaw, as Faustina and Crescentia sat drinking some tea, Faustina leaned forward and opened her heart to her dearest friend. "Sister, do you know what? I have promised Jesus that I shall refuse Him nothing, that I shall do whatever He asks of me."

Sister Crescentia smiled warmly and grabbed the hand of her good friend. She nodded, acknowledging that she understood what Faustina was saying. But Crescentia looked into those gray-green eyes. What Faustina had said was what anyone really should say. No one who really believed in Jesus should refuse Him anything. But Crescentia knew that her dear friend Faustina had every intention of keeping her word.

Sister Placida Putyra, like Sister Crescentia, was also immediately drawn to Sister Faustina. She was struck by the way that Sister Faustina always advocated praying for particular groups and intentions — the Polish army, miners, sailors, etc.

"I often wondered where she got these ideas from," observed Sister Placida later, "because I felt that in praying for everyone, I was including in that intention the various groups of people." But Faustina insisted that focusing one's prayer was more effective. And she often reminded her fellow novices that they should be vigilant in praying for the salvation of others.

Faustina also enjoyed her assignment in the kitchen. She liked keeping things spotlessly clean and really invested herself in preparing tasty dishes. "She said that we should always cook as if Jesus Himself, or the bishop, were coming to a meal," a fellow novice recalled.

Sister Faustina gave herself fully to whatever she was doing. When she worked, she worked diligently, never breaking the silence unless permission to do so had been given. And during recreation periods, she enjoyed the fellowship, and many of her fellow novices tried to sit near her. Faustina was animated, happy, positive about life and about the religious commitment they were all making.

Sister Faustina was a natural contemplative. Once her job in the kitchen was done, she could not resist the impulse to go to the chapel. She loved to pray, to spend time with God. In fact, she had already learned in her first convent years how to pray — even as she peeled potatoes, hoed in the garden, or washed sheets in the laundry room.

When the novices occasionally went outdoors for recreation, Sister Faustina would often throw her hands up to heaven and joyfully shout: "O infinitely good God, how marvelous are your works!" There was something deeply joyful and irrepressible about her.

But some of the novices remember that this young nun could also be direct and uncompromising when the situation called for it.

Once, Faustina was working in the kitchen when three older sisters laughed and chatted about the convent confessors in an uncomplimentary way. Though she was still only a novice, Sister Faustina corrected them, saying, "Excuse me, but Jesus does not like it. Please finish your conversation, Sisters." Another novice, in the kitchen to get some water, was impressed with Faustina's courage in reproving professed sisters.

In the spring of 1927, as her diary later explained, a period of discouraging darkness descended upon her. A "dark night of the soul" sabotaged the new peace she'd found in the convent. She called this terrible spiritual trial a "shadow over my soul. I felt no consolation in prayer; I had to make a great effort to meditate; fear began to sweep over me. Going deeper into myself, I could find nothing but great misery. I could also clearly see the great holiness of God. I did not dare to raise my eyes to Him, but reduced myself to dust under His feet and begged for mercy."

Mother Mary Joseph understood what was happening to Sister Faustina. This spiritual suffering is well-known to spiritual directors. It is part of the spiritual life, bringing a person into closer union with the Lord. God also uses it to purify and prepare a person whom He has chosen for a special mission. Mother encouraged her to persist in prayer. God would lift this curtain of darkness from her, but trust and faithfulness were needed in the meantime. "Know, dear Sister," the directress of novices told the heavy-hearted Faustina, "that God has chosen you for great sanctity. This is a sign that God wants to have you very close to Himself in Heaven. Have great trust in the Lord Jesus."

But as the darkness went on, day after day, it was so hard for the young woman from Glogowiec. She soon felt rejected by God. Since the age of seven she had known that Jesus was calling her to Himself. She had defied her parents and jeopardized their affection to enter the convent. And now, this same Lord seemed to be deaf to her anguished pleading.

One day, Faustina awoke and was putting herself in God's presence when she suddenly felt a wave of despair rush in upon her. There was, she wrote, "complete darkness in the soul. I fought as best I could till noon. In the afternoon, truly deadly fears began to seize me; my physical strength began to leave me."

Experiencing an abandonment and terror which approximated hell, the young woman soon collapsed in her cell in the dormitory. She had no strength to rise or call out. When another novice, Sister Placida, came into Faustina's cell and found her in such torment, she ran for Mother Mary Joseph.

"In the name of holy obedience, get up from the ground," the directress commanded when she saw her. A mysterious power then raised up Faustina to face Mother Mary Joseph. The sister's labored breathing and pale face testified to her trauma. But the older nun understood what had happened. With great kindness and gentle words, she reminded her to have great confidence in God even during such torturing trials.

These trials, however, were far from over. There was only a short period of relief that day. Then, as she noted, "my soul began to agonize again in a terrible darkness. I felt that I was in the power of the Just God, and that I was the object of His indignation." Faustina had no control over this spiritual descent, which seemed to be pulling her further and further into a pit. She struggled to claw her way out through constant appeals to the mercy of God and to His Mother. But as soon as she had risen a bit from her dark hole, she fell back down again.

One day, she said, "A terrible hatred began to break out in my soul, a hatred for all that is holy and divine. It seemed to me that these spiritual torments would be my lot for the rest of my life." More than once, she battled blasphemous thoughts during Mass. Even the thought of making her temporary vows — scheduled for the spring of 1928 — filled her with fear.

Like a shipwrecked person floundering in a stormy sea, she threw herself onto the planks she found within her reach. Devotion to the Blessed Sacrament and her faith in the mercy of Jesus kept her from sinking. And eventually, after many painful months, they carried her to shore. Fortunately, her directress of novices and her confessor pushed those planks toward her. Faustina believed that her confessor did not understand what she was going through. She would weep after confessions and was surprised when the penances he assigned her included reciting the "Te Deum" or the "Magnificat," running fast around the garden in the evening, or laughing out loud ten times a day.

In the midst of this ocean of darkness, God spoke to the young nun but there were, as yet, no words of comfort, no relief for the rejection she felt from Him.

After months of this, there were deep shadows under Faustina's blood-shot eyes.

She was pale and physically so weakened that her superiors relieved her of her kitchen assignments and all but the simplest obligations for prayer. At the same time, some of her sisters were wondering if her sufferings weren't faked. And their murmuring about her tricks occasionally reached her ears, adding to her grief.

On Good Friday in 1928, the young nun's months of agonized suffering were relieved, but only momentarily. For a short, searing moment or two, she understood how much Jesus had suffered for her and how much He loved her. Then, the comfort was again withdrawn. And though Faustina regretted that the sense of His love had not remained longer, she held onto the memory of it.

For about six months after professing her vows, Sister Faustina still suffered great spiritual trials. The dark weight of unworthiness seemed to blanket her natural joy and optimism — just as it had during her novitiate. She still endured the agonizing sense that she was rejected by heaven and that God would never again pull her into His loving and intimate embrace. But, in many ways, there was a glimmer of light and hope in the "dark night of the soul" which she continued to endure. Faustina was no longer sunk in the hopeless pit of isolation. She could see that — now and then — God was again reaching out to her.

But those long months of darkness were torturous. "Only one who has lived through similar moments can understand how terrible is this torment of the soul," she wrote in her diary years later. Unfortunately, neither the superiors nor the confessors who counseled Sister Faustina told her that what she had experienced was a "normal" phenomenon for those who come very close to God.

Shortly after Easter, on April 30, Sister Mary Faustina made her first vows. She was very happy that day. The cloud of suffering was lifted for a while. Faustina was also overjoyed to see her parents. They had traveled from Glogowiec for the ceremony.

It had been over five years since Stanislaus and Marianna had seen their favorite child, the daughter they treasured so much. But they were not prepared for what they beheld in Sister Mary Faustina. They had come, still hoping to persuade her to return home. But the glow of joy and fulfillment in her was undeniable. Seeing her so happy softened their hearts and changed their minds.

"As she is in love with Jesus, let us leave her there," Stanislaus said, at one point, shaking his head in awe. "This is the will of God." And Sister Faustina saw that her parents were now beginning to understand her calling. She walked privately with them in the convent garden. For a while, she said nothing and prayed silently, asking God what she could say to settle their hearts. She knew that her parents still wanted to see her as a happy wife and mother. Before anyone else, her mother and father had seen how good she was with children.

"You see, Daddy," the daughter finally said, turning to face her father, "the One Whose bride I am is my husband and your son-in-law." Stanislaus was very touched by this statement, and when he told others about it later, he wept.

On October 31, 1928, Sister Faustina returned to Warsaw, to the motherhouse on Zytnia Street. She was assigned to kitchen duty, and was very happy about it. This was her first assignment after her profession. She was eager to begin to serve the congregation more actively. But almost immediately, the twenty-three-year old sister became ill and was confined to the infirmary. She received good medical care and plenty of attention from her superiors, but when she continued to be ill for more than a month, some of the other nuns began to wonder and gossip about this "different nun." Could Faustina really be as ill as she said she was? How could any young nun be that ill? Wasn't she trying to get special attention or special privileges?

Convent walls also have "ears." By the end of November, the young patient had heard most of the rumors circulating about her. The charges and insinuations hurt her deeply. She really wanted to work. She longed to be active and to do her part for her new community of sisters. She was so grateful to be professed as a sister of Our Lady of Mercy. It bothered her that many of her fellow sisters suspected that she was a lazy complainer. In fact, the snide and nasty backbiting which hurt her feelings would have been found in just about any community. People talk, and plenty of talk isn't really motivated by a need to communicate.

Mother Michael Moraczewska, the new Superior General, tried to encourage Sister Faustina when she visited her one day. The long drawn-out sickness was strange, but it didn't suggest that this young woman was a malingerer, a loafer. "Sister, along your path, sufferings just spring up out of the ground," she noted. "I look upon you, Sister, as one crucified. But I can see that Jesus has some business in this."

Though Faustina was so grateful that Mother Michael trusted her, she began to doubt herself. Isn't it true, she told Jesus in prayer, that she was burdening her community? Then an older sister told the young nun that she was deluding herself about a close relationship with Jesus. After all, she informed Faustina, God only honors saints with such privileges!

"Jesus, are You not an illusion?" the beleaguered sister asked the Lord one morning. "My love deceives no one," Jesus told her. She did not have to be concerned about testing the authenticity of her call. There was nothing false, veiled, or cloudy about God's love. It would be as bright, clear, and warm as the sun itself.

Throughout 1929, however, Sister Faustina suffered greatly. As a good religious, the sister tried to open her heart and mind to her superiors about her visions and messages from God. After a time, one superior who had been supportive began to doubt the truth of Faustina's visions and conversations with the Lord. "I fear for you, Sister," she told Faustina. "It's impossible that God should commune with His creatures in such a way. You'd better go and seek the advice of a priest."

But the advice which Faustina received from priests didn't settle her anxieties. In fact, the poor sister was sent running back and forth between them and had no peace or help from her counselors. The pastoral care she received from her superiors and confessors seemed to reinforce her doubts and insecurities. But the counseling was probably as good as anyone could have provided. Faustina's needs and the careful discernment which prudent superiors exercised were at odds. Faustina needed help immediately. Those who had pastoral responsibility for her wanted to test the messages she was giving them.

And just when it seemed that matters couldn't get any worse, they did. As the young sister regained her health and settled into a more normal schedule in the large motherhouse community, her fellow sisters had a chance to study her. She had been gone for two years for her novitiate. They watched her closely now, having heard rumors of her close friendship with God. It was very soon apparent to the whole house that she was "different." Some sisters maintained that this "difference" was that Sister Faustina was completely devoted to God. But other rumors — damaging rumors and innuendoes — began to suggest that Sister Faustina might be "possessed."

Sister Faustina was still quite young. This gossiping had a negative effect upon her. For weeks after her recovery, she had doubts about her visions and revelations. She would tell the Lord, "Jesus, I am afraid of You; could You not be some kind of a phantasm?"

But now heaven tried to reassure her. Her visions were not the product of hallucinations. And gradually, the sister could not deny them. She received them and responded to them with complete obedience.

Several times during this period in Warsaw, Sister Faustina was asked by Jesus and His Mother to pray for Poland. Once, Jesus told her to ask for permission to pray for Poland for an hour a day during a nine-day novena. She was to unite her prayers with those of the Blessed Mother. Faustina went immediately to Mother Michael to ask. Mother Michael agreed to the novena, but told Faustina that she couldn't pray for a full hour a day — only the time she had after her duties were fulfilled.

On the seventh day of the novena for Poland, Sister saw the Mother of God dressed in a bright robe, standing between heaven and earth. Mary was praying, looking towards heaven. Fiery rays were coming from her heart, and some of those rays were touching Poland.

The request that Faustina intercede for Poland was repeated later. This time, Jesus showed Faustina that Warsaw, the most beautiful city in Poland, would be punished like the ancient cities of Sodom and Gomorrah for its sins. The little sister shuddered when she saw the horror and destruction and began to intercede to avert the punishment. Following another novena of seven days, she saw Christ bless her land by tracing a cross over it. Praying for Poland was part of her daily prayer from then on.

One day while praying in the chapel, Sister Faustina was thinking about the mystery of the Trinity. She'd had little religious training as a child, and only as a novice had she heard or read any teachings on the Triune God. Suddenly, she saw a light which had three sources. Out of the light came words which appeared like bolts of lightning and encircled heaven and earth. Not understanding any of this, the young woman became very sad.

Then, Jesus appeared in the midst of the light. From the central light came the words, "Who God is in His Essence, no one will fathom, neither the mind of Angels nor of man." Then Jesus told Faustina, "Get to know God by contemplating His attributes."

It was a profound theology lesson for the young nun who'd only had three brief semesters of formal schooling. Contemplating the godhead by meditating on His attributes — that was what this kitchen sister was commissioned to do. And soon, she would be contemplating the boundless, saving mercy of God. Sister Mary Faustina did not yet realize it, but it was this attribute — the mercy of God — which she was called to share with a tortured world.

Early in the morning on February 21, 1929, Sister Faustina had her small suitcase packed. She was waiting by the convent door which she had first entered almost seven years earlier. Waiting patiently for her companion, she looked around her, wondering how long she would be away from this "home" on Zytnia Street.

Sister Faustina smiled warmly when the Mother Superior, Mother Michael, entered the hallway to bless her and bid her "good-bye." And very soon, accompanied to the train station by her companion, she was on her way. She was to travel more than two hundred twenty miles to the northwest to the congregation's house in Vilnius, Poland (now in Lithuania). Sister Faustina was to replace Sister Petronela, who worked in the kitchen in Vilnius. It was time for Sister Petronela to return to the motherhouse to prepare for her perpetual vows.

Nonetheless, if Sister Faustina had known then about the many transfers which would move her from convent to convent in coming months, she might not have been so relaxed as the Vilnius train rocked her gently back and forth on the twenty-first day of February. Memories of another train may have preoccupied her. Perhaps she recalled a summer day when she'd been a tearful teenager who wept most of the way to Warsaw. Then, knowing no one, she'd stepped down onto the dusty, hot platform and into her destiny. Helena had wandered for a while, but the Lord had very soon directed her.

When Sister Faustina arrived in Vilnius, it was terribly cold. Snow crunched under her boots and the biting wind, blowing up off the Wilia River, seemed to take her breath away. With determination, the new cook made her way down the city's medieval streets to her convent. And when the young woman finally dropped into her cot after a visit to the convent chapel later that night, her feet still felt like blocks of ice.

© Marians of the Immaculate Conception

The convent and bakery of the motherhouse in Plock, where Blessed Faustina received the first vision of Jesus as The Divine Mercy.

6

The Divine Mercy Image

"I desire that this image be venerated, first in your chapel, and [then] throughout the world. I promise that the soul that will venerate this image will not perish" — Words of Jesus to Faustina,
Diary, 47.

As the 1930s began, Europe was sliding into a cataclysmic second world war. The seventy-two-year-old pontiff, Pope Pius XI, saw that the treaties which followed World War I had left many European countries edgy and angry. The seeds for a new war were sprouting.

Polish Catholics knew the Pope from his service as the papal nuncio to Poland from 1918 to 1921. Archbishop Achille Ratti had been a good friend in Warsaw when Poland was being reborn as a nation. In his younger days, Ratti had been an avid mountain climber and shared the Polish love of nature and the outdoor life. And all of Poland had seen Ratti's faith and courage. This Vatican diplomat stayed in Warsaw when Communist soldiers, led by Trotsky, tried to overtake the capital, only to be defeated by Poland's forces.

In 1922, Archbishop Ratti had become pope, and the Poles had listened more carefully than ever to news from Rome. In 1925, the pope established the feast of Christ the King. In that same year, he had also canonized Thérèse of Lisieux, an animated, charming Carmelite nun who'd found a "little way" to holiness and perfection. Three years later, in 1928, this pope wrote an encyclical letter, *Miserentissimus Redemptor*, on reparation to the Sacred Heart of Jesus.

Sister Mary Faustina, living at the motherhouse in the first months of 1930, heard about the Holy Father's deep devotion to Jesus. Her own deep devotion to Jesus was her only consolation now. While assigned to work in the garden and the kitchen, she became ill again. And yet, she was slowly realizing that there was a reason for these illnesses though they sabotaged her hope of serving her community.

"Physical weakness was for me a school of patience," she later wrote about this period. "Only Jesus knows how many efforts of will I had to make to fulfill my duty. In order to purify a soul, Jesus uses whatever instruments He likes. My soul underwent a complete abandonment on the part of creatures; often my best intentions were misinterpreted by the sisters, a type of suffering which is most painful; but God allows it, and we must accept it because in this way we become more like Jesus."

Why was this estrangement so agonizing for a twenty-five-year-old who was self-assured and independent by nature? Sister Faustina was outgoing, sociable, enthusiastic, and eager to do what was expected of her. As a child, Helena had always attempted to be obedient. She tried to rise to the expectations her parents and teachers had for her. Now she was professed in the congregation to which the Lord had directed her.

Like Thérèse of Lisieux, she had wanted to be a missionary. She longed to share her faith with the world in an active way. She wanted to live out the vocation which heaven apparently planned. At this point in time, she didn't see how she could be what she was intended to be — a productive sister among the Sisters of Our Lady of Mercy.

One problem was the puzzled and guarded reaction of many sisters to this unique personality. The sister from Glogowiec made some nuns uncomfortable. Some of them even resented her. Sister Faustina believed that no sister should ever question the authority of her superiors. Some of her peers thought that her position — occasionally shared during recreation — was "too rigid." Faustina had also told her superiors about some sisters who were in sinful situations. She was told by the Lord to share these visions.

"On one occasion I saw two sisters who were about to enter hell. A terrible agony tore my soul; I prayed to God for them, and Jesus said to me: 'Go to Mother Superior and tell her that those two sisters are in danger of committing a mortal sin.' The next day I told this to the Superior. One of them had already repented with great fervor and the other was going through a great struggle."

Sister Mary Faustina was exceptional in her devotion to prayer and obedience. This quality of extraordinary devotion often led to misunderstandings. Many of her peers liked her. But at times, they didn't know what to make of her style of prayer, her spiritual intensity, her gifts. She was, after all, a nun of the second choir, not the first. There were no expectations that a nun of the second choir would lead a contemplative life of prayer. She was supposed to pray largely through her work in the garden, the kitchen, the laundry. When those jobs were done, there was certainly time for a second-choir nun to pray. Helena had been told this many times as a postulant and as a novice. Yet Faustina's spiritual gifts intimidated those around her. They didn't know that she experienced visions and saw future events as clearly as one might see the sunset.

Sister Faustina's immediate superiors knew about her spiritual life, but they had also become more guarded in response to her claims of heavenly visions and messages. Her accounts often seemed unbelievable and yet she was clearly sincere, devout, prayerful. So for a time, Faustina was viewed as a well-meaning but delusional young woman. Every convent had seen such cases. The nuns in charge of her periodically threw up their hands in frustration. They weren't sure they knew how to handle her and neither did Faustina's confessors.

The young nun was at her wit's end. She was extremely conscientious in the observance of her vow of obedience. She believed that she should be open and honest in telling her superiors about her spiritual life. How else could they guide her? But she found that her honesty often generated misunderstanding. The language of the spirit was difficult to translate. Faustina learned this lesson the hard way.

"There was one thing which I could not understand for a long time: Jesus ordered me to tell everything to my Superiors, but my Superiors did not believe what I said and treated me with pity as though I was being deluded or was imagining things."

Faustina's frequent transfers from one convent to another also didn't help the situation. It would have been very difficult for her to settle down, and for her superiors to get to know her even in the best circumstances. In fact, she was transferred much more often than other sisters. Sister Faustina was transferred frequently because she made no complaints and never voiced objections to decisions affecting her. Many of the other sisters grumbled about transfers or even resisted being moved. But the difficulties some other sisters had with the young nun, and her superiors' perplexity about how best to direct her, may also have contributed to Sister Faustina's frequent transfers.

This friendly sister had never asked for phenomenal events in her life. But she did accept them as coming from God. The Lord Jesus was communicating with her in extraordinary ways. Faustina wisely prayed for a spiritual director who could finally understand and guide her.

In May or June of 1930, Sister Faustina was again reassigned. This time, she packed her suitcase and headed for Plock, a city about one hundred miles northwest of Warsaw. Plock was a much smaller city than Warsaw and had once been a center of scholarly activity. The brick convent of the

Sisters of Our Lady of Mercy stood right on the street and the order's Guardian Angel Home was nearby on Old Market Square.

Sister Faustina was again given kitchen work to do. In this convent, however, the kitchen was long and narrow. It was the corridor through which everyone traveled in and out of the house. The constant coming and going in the midst of the cooks' activities was difficult. Interruptions were the norm throughout the day. She did not complain about her long, grueling days, but Sister Faustina soon became ill and unable to do her work.

The Mother Superior at Plock consulted with the doctors. They shook their heads in bewilderment. Tuberculosis — the likely answer — is difficult to diagnose in its early stages. The airborne bacterial infection may have entered her body years earlier. Such an infection can remain dormant and then begin to slowly invade the rest of the body through the lymphatic system. In any case, Faustina's doctors could not find a specific cause for her weakness and fatigue. They advised rest for her.

So, in the fall of 1930, the ailing cook was sent for rest to the sisters' farm at the nearby village of Biala. It was quiet there and her job as cook wasn't demanding at all. The farm was run by just three sisters, including the cook. Occasionally at Biala there were a few visiting nuns or girls to entertain. People loved to come to this country house to celebrate holidays.

The fresh air and the golden fields of wheat and rye did do Sister Faustina some good. She soon felt at home, relaxed. She was no longer scrutinized at every turn by dozens of eyes. Her workload was lighter than at Plock, though she still put in a full day of work.

Generously, Sister Faustina socialized and played quoits and other games with the wards — the young women and girls in the care of the order. The girls loved her for the way she told stories and for the spirited way she would roll back her sleeves to toss the ring towards the stake during quoits.

At age twenty-five, she was close enough to the girls in age. But they could also see that she was mature, controlled, well-balanced, and happy. And there was a deep and powerful spirituality in her that attracted them.

"Mother, Sister Faustina has lots of intelligence and even more heart," wrote one young girl named Ursula. "After all she works hard in the kitchen, so she could have just rested in the shade of a tree, but to give us pleasure, she would play with us."

Another of the girls recalled that Sister Faustina always treated them with great respect. When the wards behaved in a rude manner, "Sister Faustina never asked us to apologize to her, and she always behaved kindly and lovingly to everyone she had contact with, whether she had been treated unpleasantly or with courtesy."

Faustina also often asked the girls if they were hungry. She knew what it was like to be worried about getting enough to eat. She wanted the girls to be satisfied, secure, well-fed. They should know the blessings of a loving home. If their physical needs were taken care of, they would be more ready to see that the source of every good thing was God.

By Christmas, it was clear that Sister Faustina was regaining her strength. There was good color in her face now, and the gray-green eyes sparkled. She enjoyed her walks to the barnyard, where she'd already befriended the cows, the chickens, and a stray cat or two. When she could, she'd bundle up against the winter wind and walk around the fields, thinking perhaps of Glogowiec and the farm where she'd grown up.

Soon, Sister Faustina was back at the large convent at Plock. This time, however, she wasn't given any kitchen duties — only work in the convent bakery and store. She enjoyed meeting people in the store and always served her customers with a smile. She'd hand them a warm loaf of rye bread or some rolls with a friendly greeting and cheerful efficiency. To be honest, even the lighter workload was extremely tiring for her. She was often totally worn-out at the end of the day. But Sister Faustina was determined to persist and carry out her job.

Most nights, Sister Faustina was exhausted when she got into her narrow cot in her cell. As she had since childhood, she often awoke during the night and got up to pray. There was so much to tell Jesus. And, there were so many things that He had to tell her. The intimacy she knew with Jesus had grown deeper since those trying months of darkness during her novitiate.

Just after the New Year of 1931, Sister Faustina told Jesus that she would suffer anything for Him. Years later, she remembered the intensity with which she had told the Lord of her total dedication.

"In comparison with You, everything is nothing," she wrote. "Sufferings, adversities, humiliations, failures and suspicions that have come my way are splinters that keep alive the fire of my love for You, O Jesus. I want never to be rewarded for my effort and my good actions. You Yourself, Jesus, are my only reward; You are enough, O Treasure of my heart!"

Sister Faustina Kowalska had no idea that Jesus, the Treasure of her heart, would soon be taking her at her word.

On the evening of February 22, 1931, Faustina went to her cell, wearied after a busy day in the bakery. The other sisters of the house were also going to bed after community prayer in the chapel.

Suddenly, the young woman saw "the Lord Jesus clothed in a white garment." The brightness of His image stole her breath for a moment. Her heart began to race. Jesus was so glorious and yet so loving. This vision would bring the most important message that Sister Faustina had ever received, and she sensed it right away.

When she wrote about this apparition in her diary more than three years later, what she saw and heard was as fresh as if it had happened the day before. Faustina noticed the hands of Jesus, first of all.

"One hand [was] raised in the gesture of blessing, the other was touching the garment at the breast. From beneath the garment, slightly drawn aside at the breast, there were emanating two large rays, one red, the other pale. In silence I kept my gaze fixed on the Lord. After a while, Jesus said to me, 'Paint an image according to the pattern you see, with the signature: Jesus, I trust in You.' "

As the young woman stared at the image, she must have asked herself what Jesus meant by telling her to "paint an image." She had no skills as a painter; she was no artist. What could He mean? Faustina sighed, her heart full of love for this Savior. It was a lover's sigh. As a little girl, she had wondered how she could ever love Him any more. At this moment, gazing at His heart, she sensed that this same Jesus was showing her a picture of His love for her and for the world. Faustina's heart seemed in danger of bursting. She was so very happy, so completely ecstatic. But Jesus had more mysterious things to tell her and to ask of her.

"I desire that this image be venerated, first in your chapel, and [then] throughout the world. I promise that the soul that will venerate this image will not perish. I also promise victory over [its] enemies already here on earth, especially at the hour of death. I myself," Jesus concluded, "will defend it as My own glory."

When the Lord had finished speaking, His image dissolved into the hushed darkness of the convent dormitory. Faustina's own heart still thumped wildly in her own chest. She dropped to her knees to pray in thanksgiving, then in joy. Tears washed quietly down her smooth, white cheeks to cling to her chin and jaw. As she wiped them away, washing her face with them, she stood once more and bowed to the place where He had appeared.

And then, climbing into bed, Sister Faustina spent the night listening to the many different rhythms of her sisters breathing all around her. The bakery nun didn't sleep much that night. Jesus had some very large tasks for her to do. How could she do them? Who would believe the nun whom many of her sleeping sisters called "hysterical" and "delusional." And how could she — a simple nun of the second choir — paint a masterpiece of the Lord Jesus?

Sister Faustina simply didn't know how any of it could be done. But she did understand intuitively that this vision would shape her future as a religious, as a beloved spouse of Jesus. She would have to see to it that His will would be done. And she drew strength, from those words He wanted inscribed at the bottom of the image: "*Jezu, Ufam Tobie*" — "Jesus, I trust in You."

7

How to Paint an Image

*"Paint an image according to the pattern you see. . ." — Words of Jesus to Faustina, **Diary, 47**.*

On February 23, 1931, Sister Faustina turned those words over and over in her mind. The day was cold, and lack of sleep the night before made her thin frame tremble just a bit. She was warm only when she stood right next to the bakery ovens. She went about her duties with a faint smile on her face, a distant look in her eyes. No one would have noticed anything different about the "mysterious" Faustina.

But within her, there was something new going on. This sister imagined herself painting — painting on a huge canvas. She visualized herself painting a magnificent image of her magnificent Jesus. But how? She had no skills whatsoever to paint, or even to draw. How could it be done?

Sister Faustina had no problem remembering the "pattern" — the way Jesus looked. The colors of the rays radiating from His chest. The angle of His hand raised for blessing. The loving gaze of His eyes. She had an excellent memory, and her sisters had noticed that she never needed to be told anything twice. This image of Christ was already "painted" forever in her memory.

But how should she "paint" it for others to see?

As soon as it was possible, Sister Faustina brought the matter to her confessor at the convent. The convent in Plock had three regular confessors: Monsignor Adolf Modzelewski, Monsignor Lewis Wilkonski, and Father Waclaw Jezusek. She told one of these men about the vision and the command Christ had given to her to paint the image and then display it.

The priest told her, "Certainly, paint God's image in your soul." Her confessor thought that the words of Jesus had been symbolic — metaphors for the nun. Wondering if that could be the answer, Faustina left the confessional, only to hear Jesus responding in a convent corridor.

"My image is already in your soul," He said. "I desire that there be a Feast of Mercy. I want this image, which you will paint with a brush, to be solemnly blessed on the first Sunday after Easter; that Sunday is to be the Feast of Mercy." Jesus also said that He wanted priests to proclaim this great Feast of Mercy to sinners, who should not be afraid to approach Him. Then, Jesus said that "distrust on the part of souls is tearing at My insides. The distrust of a chosen soul causes Me even greater pain."

Sister Mary Faustina cringed at those words. She did not want to be one of the souls who distrusted the Lord, who gave Him pain. Yet she still did not know how this painted image of Jesus was to be created. Would God somehow endow her with the talent, the knowledge, and the confidence that she lacked? She went to discuss it with the Mother Superior.

Forty-one-year-old Mother Rose Klobukowski listened very carefully to the extraordinary young novice. Glancing occasionally at the huge cross which hung on the wall behind Faustina, she saw that the nun was troubled by what was being asked of her. Mother told Sister Faustina to ask for some sign from Jesus to authenticate this message. It was a cautious approach to Faustina's phenomenal report, but it wasn't a bad plan.

Jesus responded to this immediately. "I will make this all clear to the Superior by means of the graces which I will grant through this image," He reassured Sister Faustina. But she did not know when this would be. She did not know what she should do until the Lord sent the needed sign.

For many months, Sister Faustina tried to flee from this new responsibility, this new mission Jesus had given her. She told herself that it was too much for a woman with her feeble abilities, her limited education. But she quickly found that she would have no choice except to see that the image was painted.

"When I tried to run away from these interior aspirations," she wrote later in her diary, "God said to me that on the day of judgment He would demand of me a great number of souls." And the caring heart in this sister was not going to let any souls be lost because she neglected her duty.

The months of 1931 moved along. The times were unsettled, and the bakery sister with visions was unsettled too. The king of Spain was deposed and had fled into exile. Central Europe was plunged into a financial crisis, and financial difficulties were so generally desperate throughout the continent that the American president Herbert Hoover proposed a one-year moratorium on reparations and war debts.

In Germany, a millionaire named Hugenberg decided to support the Nazi Party, which by then numbered eight hundred thousand. Allied troops had left the Rhineland only the year before and the nation was in financial and political chaos. In addition to losing all of its colonies and some of its European territories — including Poznan and parts of Silesia and West Prussia to Poland — Germany was required to pay $33 million. Adolf Hitler, head of the Nazi Party, was growing more and more powerful.

In Poland, Jozef Pilsudski established a right-wing government as he tried to bring some stability to a country which had been separated into three regions for more than a century. In 1926, Pilsudski had taken complete control of the government, dismissing the other political parties and ending any Polish pretense to democracy. To "President" Pilsudski, it seemed that Poland needed someone in absolute control to lead it in the right direction.

Direction of a much different sort was precisely what Sister Faustina was seeking. Her commission was to "paint an image" of Jesus, but directing her toward that goal just didn't make sense to her counselors. So, after a few months, she began to seek some help from others. Sister Bozena, also assigned to work in the bakery, remembered some odd questions from Faustina.

Faustina asked her friend, a first-choir nun, if she knew how to paint. She explained that she needed a picture of Jesus. She promised to give her the brush and paints.

"I answered that I could not paint, I had never done so and could not undertake it," recalled Sister Bozena. Then Bozena offered to give her a picture of Jesus, but Faustina politely declined, begging the other nun to be discreet and say nothing to others of her request.

Despite the discreet silence which Sister Bozena kept, the convent was soon buzzing with rumors. Sister Faustina had asked some other sisters about doing a painting for her. When no one could help, she began to sketch an outline on a canvas with charcoal.

"Did you hear — Jesus appeared to Faustina?" the nuns whispered to one other in the corridors. "Does Sister Faustina really think she had a vision?" Some of the sisters were simply aghast; some were offended by the suggestion. But almost all of them tried to get more information about the matter.

Sister Aloiza asked the sister who shared a bedroom with Faustina if she'd ever heard the "visionary" talking with anyone. Aloiza had heard a rumor that Faustina talked with Jesus at night. But Sister Faustina's dormitory neighbor hadn't heard any such thing. "I answered that I had not heard this. We shared a bedroom; the beds were separated by curtains."

"More than once I was seized with laughter when I learned they would not even leave my bed alone," Sister Faustina wrote. "One of the sisters herself told me that she came to observe me in my cell every evening to see how I behave in it."

Sister Faustina gritted her teeth and remained silent in the midst of rumors, snickers, and curious inquisitors. A few sisters believed in Faustina, and one nun came to her and told her: "I've heard them say that you are a fantasist, Sister, and that you've been having visions. My poor Sister, defend yourself in this matter."

"My only desire," the beleaguered Sister Faustina wrote later in her diary, "was that some priest would say this one word to me: 'Be at peace, you are on the right road,' or 'Reject all this for it does not come from God.' But I could not find such a priest who was sufficiently sure of himself to give me a definite opinion in the name of the Lord." In fact, one priest told her that he was somewhat afraid to hear her confession.

Did twenty-six-year-old Sister Faustina ever have any regrets that she had entered religious life? Did she wonder why so many of the Sisters of Our Lady of Mercy could not resist judging her? It's hard to imagine that such thoughts didn't force themselves upon her as she tried to go about her daily duties — kneading bread, sweeping the flour in the bake shop, counting the zlotys at the end of the day.

One day, she suffered the greatest humiliation yet. It came from one of the superiors at Plock — probably seventy-three-year-old Mother Jane Bartkiewicz.

Faustina had gone to talk to Mother Jane. She bared her soul, explaining how anxious she felt about fulfilling the command from Jesus to paint His image. The slender sister complained that she had no talent to do such a painting and could find no one who could. Faustina looked at her superior, hoping that she had some words of advice. Instead, the older woman exploded in anger.

"You queer, hysterical visionary," she thundered, "get out of this room; go on with you, Sister!" Mother Jane continued to hurl loud and disparaging remarks at the cringing Faustina, who moved out of the room as quickly as her young legs could take her. As the door closed on the elderly nun's bellowing, a wave of humiliation washed over the well-meaning and sincere Faustina. Her cheeks were aflame, her forehead sweating. She wanted to hurry, melt into the floor, and disappear.

The sister returned almost immediately to her daily chores in the bakery. She concentrated on concealing her pain and humiliation. "There is no need for the other sisters to know about Mother's anger with me," she told herself. "What good would that do?" But after evening prayer, Sister Faustina retreated to her room and collapsed, face down, in tears. She had never been so wounded by another person's words and expressions of scorn. And these words had come from her superior in religion!

Quite quickly the sense of shame was mixed with feelings of discouragement. Why should she try to communicate the Lord's requests when everything she said and did was misinterpreted or even condemned? The feelings of discouragement sank a little lower, deeper into her heart.

"Jesus, Jesus, I cannot go on any longer," she cried, tasting the salty tears in her hands. She was desperate and suddenly terribly afraid. What would she do if no one ever believed her again?

At that low moment, with her face on the floor, Jesus spoke in her heart. "Do not fear; I am with you," He consoled her. It was what she needed to hear. He did not say that she would never again be discouraged or misunderstood. But Faustina was once again assured that she would not suffer these things without Him. A peace was poured into her soul, and her tense and fractured spirit regained some composure. Her body relaxed and she rose from the floor, wiping her face with the back of her hand. She understood something more: She should never again surrender to such crippling grief, to such paralyzing negativity. No matter what!

Nonetheless, during the rest of 1931, little changed in the emotional climate in the big convent at Plock. Sister Faustina was tense, knowing that she was watched — even while she was sleeping. And as she climbed the stairs or left the bakery ovens to get some more flour or sugar from the pantry, she heard the whispers. She didn't have to listen to know what was being said about her.

From time to time, the feeling of isolation nudged her back into a gray gloominess. In such a mood, she one day reminded Jesus that her superiors said that phantoms and illusions may have deceived her. She understood that it was possible for Satan to fool her and lead her astray. And during her prayer time, on another day, Sister Faustina impulsively challenged her Lord.

"If You are my Lord, I beg You to bless me," she said. Immediately Faustina saw Jesus make a large sign of the cross over her. She also signed herself, sighing with relief. The young nun didn't feel quite right, putting Jesus to the test. But when she did, He always reassured her with His presence. In a very painful way, Sister Faustina Kowalska was slowly discovering that Jesus was the only one she could completely trust.

Throughout the rest of 1931 and well into 1932, the young sister from Glogowiec suffered greatly. In many ways, her sisters at Plock valued her as a model nun. And yet everyone conceded that she was different, separated from them by her spiritual life, and — now, more than ever — by her rumored visions.

Some of the sisters dubbed her "the princess." It was a strange title for a young woman who'd grown up in poverty. It didn't seem to fit someone who had only three semesters of schooling and who never had a Sunday dress of her own until she was fifteen.

"The princess." When Helen Kowalska — Sister Mary Faustina — heard herself called that name, it hurt. She had never tried to raise herself above her sisters. Indeed, she didn't think of herself in those exalted terms.

And yet, the Lord Jesus — the King of all Creation — had given His image to her to share with the world. Faustina understood that there was a way in which she was set apart, called, chosen. When she overheard the "princess" remark, the twenty-six-year-old sister swung around and responded to her sisters. "Yes, I am a princess," she told them, "for the royal Blood of Jesus flows in me."

That close connection with her King was to deepen even further — much further — than Sister Faustina herself could have imagined.

8

A Victim Soul

"My daughter, speak to priests about this inconceivable mercy of Mine. The flames of mercy are burning Me — clamoring to be spent; I want to keep pouring them out upon souls; souls just don't want to believe in My goodness" — Words of Jesus to Faustina, **Diary, 177**.

Throughout the first ten months of 1932, Sister Faustina felt intense discomfort whenever she passed by a certain wall in the Plock convent. The wall, it seemed, was a silent reproach.

Leaning her canvas against this wall, Faustina had tried to do what Jesus had told her to do. Jesus had said: "Paint an image according to the pattern you see, with the signature: 'Jesus, I trust in You.' " But Jesus had not told her *where* to paint the image, and He had not told her *how* to paint it. One of the sisters had instructed Sister Faustina in a few techniques that artists used in creating paintings. The would-be-painter learned that she would have to sketch out the image of Jesus before she could paint it.

With charcoal pencils, Sister Faustina had labored to rough out the outline of Jesus. Praying as she worked, she had tried to capture the strong, beautiful outline of Christ's figure. The hand raised in blessing was held at a certain angle. One foot had to be positioned well in front of the other. The eyes of Jesus had to be just so. The tunic needed to hang in rich, glowing white folds. And the glowing of pale and red rays flowing from His heart had to look like glowing showers of light.

Although Jesus had indeed painted His image in her soul, Sister Faustina could not paint it upon the canvas. She remembered every detail so well — but the memory just could not be translated to her hand, to her fingers clumsily clutching drawing tools she'd never held before.

Finally, she'd thrown down the charcoal pencil and wept. She had prayed for the talent to create the image, but it had not come. Sister Faustina could not even draw the rough outline of Jesus to her own satisfaction. There could be no glorious painting, no beautiful image from her own hand. Anxious, nervous, anguished, she wondered what Jesus thought of her failure to fulfill His command.

That "wall of reproach" and the dwindling days of the year preoccupied Sister Faustina. She knew very well that the time to prepare for her final vows was approaching. That meant that she would be transferred from Plock back to the motherhouse in Warsaw. The period of preparation was called the "third probation."

"Lord, must I leave this house with no work done to paint this image?" Time after time in private prayer in chapel, Sister Faustina whispered the question. It came from an anguished and anxious heart. She agonized over the painting she didn't know how to paint. And did Jesus want the painting venerated in the chapel in Plock? How could that happen if she was to be somewhere else? Or did He simply want it displayed wherever she was when it was completed?

The slender sister of the second choir — the one many of her peers dubbed "the princess"— had not yet found anyone who could help her sort out such questions. She still prayed deliberately and unceasingly for a spiritual advisor. There had to be a priest who could help light her path.

Without a solid, holy, and mature priest to guide her, Sister Faustina was still victimized by her doubts. Was the vision she received truly from God? On the other hand, could it not have been an elaborate but edifying daydream? Since childhood, she had longed to be missionary for the "hidden Jesus." Could this "vision" have been a projection of her own desire to share Jesus with the world? Sister Mary Faustina did not think so. But she was not totally sure.

To test herself, as she later explained in her diary, she tested Jesus periodically.

Once, Sister Faustina was in the midst of her workday and one of the wards— a girl with a troubled history — was nearby.

"At one time, when I was filled with doubts as to whether the voice I heard came from the Lord or not, I began to speak to Jesus interiorly without forming any words. Suddenly, an inner force took hold of me and I said, 'If you who commune with me and talk to me are truly my God, I beg You, O Lord, to make this ward go this very day to confession; this sign will give me reassurance.' "

At that very moment, Sister Faustina wrote, the girl asked to go to confession. Sister Faustina nodded quietly and smiled warmly at the girl. But deep in her soul, there was a private shout of joy. "Yes, yes, yes!" Jesus had answered her as specifically and as quickly as possible. The answer had come from outside of her own consciousness — from the mouth of the girl standing nearby. Faustina laughed to herself, noticing that the youngster had a quizzical expression on her face. The nun in charge of the class was even more surprised. But she immediately called a priest.

Inside, Faustina heard a voice saying: "Do you believe me now?" Yes, the vision had been a real message given to her! Yes, the Lord of heaven wanted her to produce an image of His divine mercy! What a joy and a relief to know for sure! For a short while, Sister Faustina had a certain sort of peace. But, as she later noticed, doubts periodically washed over her like waves upon the rocks.

In November of 1932, Sister Faustina said farewell to everyone at Plock and headed for Warsaw. The transfer was to return her first to the motherhouse and then to Cracow for the five-month probationary period before she professed her final vows. The twenty-seven-year-old Faustina may have felt some relief in leaving behind the community where she was so misunderstood. And yet, in that large house at Plock where she had lived for two-and-one-half years, Jesus had entrusted her with a monumental ministry.

On the day she arrived in Warsaw, Sister Faustina was immediately greeted with warmth and kindness. She was particularly happy to learn that Mother Margaret Gimbutt would be her director during the probationary period. Because Sister Faustina had not yet made a retreat, Mother Margaret dispatched her immediately to nearby Walendow, where an eight-day retreat had just begun.

Before she left Plock, however, one nun had made it very clear that she had no friendly feelings at all for Sister Faustina. This nun bluntly and coldly informed her that she would be voting to reject her in the upcoming meeting of superiors. The meeting was held to screen out nuns before they entered the probationary period that led to their final vows. Why did this nun want Sister Faustina out of the order? Faustina didn't know, but that threat chilled her to the bone. At Warsaw, she went upstairs to pack a smaller bag for the retreat and headed to the chapel with a heavy heart, a knot of fear in her throat.

At Walendow, Faustina relaxed a bit and prepared to soak in all of the peace and spiritual renewal she could get. In prayer, Jesus told her that this retreat would be different. The eight days were to be especially rich for her. The director of the retreat, an American Jesuit, Father Edmund Elter, was to help her a great deal in confession.

Just as the Lord had foretold it, the confession Sister Faustina made with Father Elter gave her great peace of mind. Father Elter was a professor of homiletics and ethics at the Gregorian University in Rome. He was then living in Warsaw, giving retreats to many religious. His soothing and carefully reasoned responses calmed Sister Faustina. She sensed that this learned man had great humility and a deep and quiet love of His Lord.

Before she went to confession, Faustina had been tempted to be silent about her vision and her Divine Mercy mission. She knew that Father Elter wouldn't continue as her confessor. There was so much to explain, and there would be no time for this priest to get to know her.

But this confession was a turning point for her. For the first time since receiving the Divine Mercy image, she was free of doubts about it. She realized what God wanted her to do and understood what she was not to do. She received great peace from the sacrament and the sensible counsel of Father Elter. He told her to trust Jesus, but to tell her superiors only what her confessor told her to tell them. What he said rang true in her heart and Sister Faustina sighed with relief.

Soon after her confession, she was strolling in the garden, feeling joyful and blessed. Suddenly, Sister Faustina's heart was filled with love for her God. In return, she was overcome by the presence of God and she sensed the Three Divine Persons dwelling in her.

The rest of the retreat went well. Life as a nun of the second choir was a very busy one. Sister Faustina was very happy to be able to spend these days quietly, prayerfully. But not all of her sisters relished the silence as she did. One night, a sister she hadn't seen for a long time came to her room and said that she had something to tell her. Wanting to maintain the silence during these retreat days, Sister Faustina said nothing. Irritated and offended, the other nun soon stalked off, calling Faustina "an eccentric."

On the last day of the retreat, after receiving Holy Communion, Sister Faustina had a vision of the Sacred Heart of Jesus. As her heart raced with excitement, the sister quietly viewed His image. She notice that the rays which shone from His heart were like the red and pale rays emanating from the breast of Jesus in the Divine Mercy image she'd seen the year before. Although it was clear what Jesus was saying, she also heard His words.

"My daughter," He said, "speak to priests about this inconceivable mercy of Mine. The flames of mercy are burning Me — clamoring to be spent; I want to keep pouring them out upon souls; souls just don't want to believe in My goodness."

A few weeks later, Sister Faustina got good news. She learned that she had been accepted for the third probation. She was surprised, since the nun who opposed her had said, "Sister, you will not be going for your third probation. I myself will see to it that you will not be permitted to make your vows."

On December 1, 1932, the third probationary period began for the sisters who would be making their final vows. In Faustina's group, there were three sisters, including herself. Each one was preparing to make a lifelong commitment to her congregation and to the Lord. It was an emotional beginning for Faustina.

At a meeting with the other probationers and with Mother Margaret Gimbutt, Sister Faustina burst into tears, thinking of the times she'd been ungrateful to God. With her two peers shaking their heads at her emotional display, Faustina wept and wept. Mother Margaret, on the other hand, understood Faustina's grief and sympathized with the sobbing young woman who loved God so fiercely.

Mother Margaret was seventy-five and she knew that Sister Faustina's heart was an honest and faithful one. A loving and perceptive woman, Mother Margaret had seen a bit of the world before she entered the convent at age thirty-six in 1893. She was a good judge of character and was not a stranger to leadership. She had been directress of novices and later served as superior of the convent in Vilnius. She won the respect and love of her sisters with humility, prayerfulness, and unfailing respect for the congregation's rules.

Mother knew that this twenty-seven-year-old nun she was directing had profound spiritual gifts. They were gifts that would set her apart as surely as the sounds of her sobbing rose above the chatter of the other young women sitting in the parlor chairs nearby. As Advent began, Sister Faustina was put to work in the vestiary, repairing clothing, sewing new items as they were needed, and distributing them to various sisters. Sister's partner, Sister Suzanne Tokarski, may have been a bit too demanding and impatient. But so too were some of the sisters to whom Faustina carried bedding and clothing. They often had her return to the vestiary for different items two or three times before they were satisfied with what she brought them.

Cheerfully remembering that every thorn prick could be suffered for love, Sister Faustina was actually happy. She had so many opportunities to practice patience and charity. But when she soon became ill and had to stay in bed, she was labeled as "lazy." Even in Warsaw, some of the sisters had heard that this second-choir nun preferred to pray all day, leaving the laundry undone, the meals uncooked.

When she felt better, Sister Faustina again threw herself fully into work and into prayer. She was very excited to be preparing for her final vows. To be fully, finally, and forever committed to Jesus! That was such a blessing, a blessing which she wanted to receive with humility.

In prayer, however, Faustina was reminding Jesus of her need for a spiritual director. She now realized that she would need an especially gifted and virtuous priest to guide her and the Divine Mercy mission which she had been given. In fact, she assumed that she would be given such a priest. She prayed for a good confessor. Her confessor would need to understand her thoroughly.

In the meantime, something new was also asked of Sister Faustina. It happened one night in the autumn or winter of 1932 during an hour of adoration. The little sister who had already suffered so much in her twenty-seven years experienced another vision. This time, however, she foresaw what was to happen in her own life. Faustina's future was instantaneously displayed before her eyes.

On this cold winter night, the years ahead were compressed and then unfurled in front of her, like a large carpet. The stunned young woman "saw" what would befall her if she chose to become a "victim soul."

A "victim soul" is a person who wishes to be as much like Jesus as possible. Since Jesus redeemed His brothers and sisters through His suffering and death, a person who wants to be like Him graciously accepts great sufferings. God, in turn, accepts this extraordinary suffering as a gift of reparation or atonement for the sinful world. Such a commitment is at the heart of the Gospel. Didn't Jesus ask His closest friends to take up a cross and follow Him?

In her vision, Faustina witnessed the deterioration of her health and watched as her young body became diseased, distorted, tormented. Then, she witnessed the accusations and attacks that others would hurl at her, her reputation, and her name in the years to come. When the vision was over, Sister Faustina's forehead was bathed in sweat. Her heart was racing with fear and dread. She had previewed all the agonies of her future life. And there were many planned for her.

"Jesus made it known to me," she later wrote, "that even if I did not give my consent to this, I could still be saved; and He would not lessen His graces, but would still continue to have the same intimate relationship with me, so that even if I did not make this sacrifice, God's generosity would not lessen thereby." But Faustina did give her consent. Her name, she realized, was to be: "sacrifice."

"You are the delight of My Heart," Jesus told her when her decision was made to accept this role. "From today on, every one of your acts, even the very smallest, will be a delight to My eyes, whatever you do." Because of the sacrifice she agreed to make, God carried her deeper into His heart. Though she later tried to describe what happened, it really couldn't be expressed in words.

"I felt that His Majesty was enveloping me. I was extraordinarily fused with God. A great mystery took place during that adoration, a mystery between the Lord and myself. It seemed to me that I would die of love [at the sight of] His glance. I spoke much to the Lord without uttering a single word. My earthly body was the same, but my soul was different; God was now living in it with the totality of His delight. This is not a feeling, but a conscious reality that nothing can obscure."

With this "different" soul, she could now see that the greatest attributes of God are love and mercy. On the day before Christmas 1932, Sister Faustina was united in spirit with the pregnant Mary. She felt what the young mother felt as the birth of her child approached. During Midnight Mass and on Christmas Day, the young nun saw the Child Jesus in the Host. He was so beautiful and so tiny. Sister Mary Faustina adored and thanked God for one of His most merciful gifts — the Incarnation. Jesus, the Son of God, became a child!

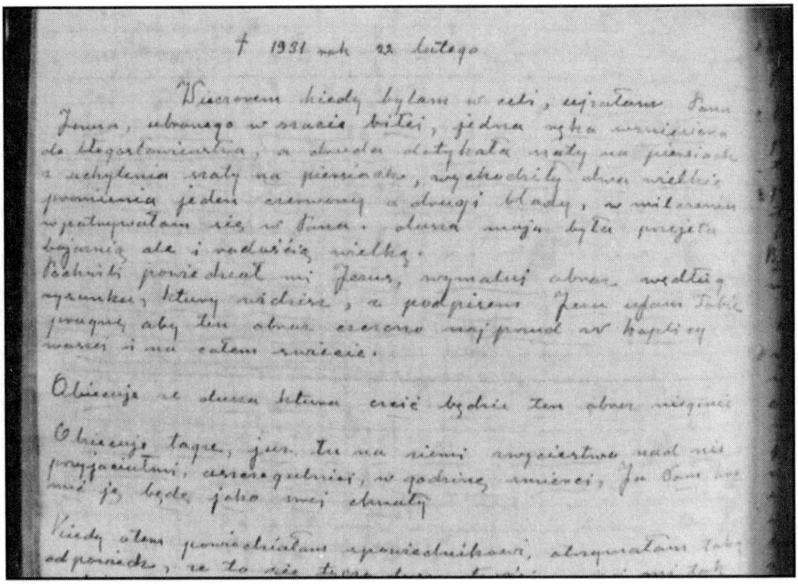

† 1931 roku 22 lutego

Wieczorem kiedy byłam w celi, ujrzałam Pana Jezusa, ubranego w szacie białej, jedna ręka wzniesiona do błogosławieństwa, a druga dotykała szaty na piersiach z uchylenia szaty na piersiach, wychodziły dwa wielkie promienia jeden czerwony a drugi blady, w milczeniu wpatrywałam się w Pana. dusza moja była przejęta bojaźnią ale i radością wielką.
Pochwili powiedział mi Jezus, wymaluj obraz według rysunku, który widzisz, z podpisem Jezu ufam Tobie pragnę aby ten obraz czczono najpierw w kaplicy waszej i na całym świecie.

Obiecuje że dusza która czcić będzie ten obraz nie zginie

Obiecuje także, już tu na ziemi zwycięstwo nad nieprzyjaciołmi, szczególniej, w godzinę śmierci, Ja Sam bronić ją będę jako swej chwały

Kiedy o tem powiedziałam spowiednikowi, otrzymałam taką odpowiedź, że to się tyczy [illegible]

A page from Faustina's diary.

9

A Diary of Mercy

*"The two rays denote Blood and Water. The pale ray stands for the
Water which makes souls righteous. The red ray stands for the
Blood which is the life of souls. These two rays issued forth from
the very depth of My tender mercy when My agonized Heart was
opened by a lance on the Cross" — Words of Jesus to Faustina,*
Diary, 299.

"Praised be Jesus Christ! Happy New Year, Sister!"

"Forever and ever. Amen! And a happy year to you, too, Sister Faustina!"

Sister Faustina would have been happy to share New Year's greetings
with the whole world on the first day of 1933. She had some wonderful
things to look forward to. She had already been given a glimpse of her
future spiritual director! She'd seen his face in a vision and knew that she'd
recognize him when the time came. She was hoping that the time would
come soon.

In the spring of 1933, Faustina also expected to make her final vows as
a Sister of Our Lady of Mercy. To prepare herself, she was trying to keep
the Great Silence all during the period of her probation. She went about her
job in the vestiary, silently sewing torn sheets, hemming slips, and darning
stockings for her sisters. She was already aware that it would be a wonderful year in which to make this great commitment to the Lord. The Christian
world was preparing to mark a unique anniversary — 1900 years since the
death of Jesus Christ.

One gloomy winter day shortly before Lent, Sister Faustina made her
way to the chapel. She had been trying to think of ways to prove her love to
the Lord as the day of her solemn vows came closer and closer. A prayer
was given to her as she lay prostrate before the altar. Jesus told her that if
she said this prayer "with a contrite heart and with faith on behalf of some
sinner, I will give him the grace of conversion."

The words of the prayer were: *"O Blood and Water, which gushed forth from the Heart of Jesus as a fount of Mercy for us, I trust in You."* Faustina immediately committed the words to memory and understood that this prayer was another tool for her mission — the interceding for souls.

As "victim soul," she also began to experience new psychological and emotional suffering. Faustina knew where her strange bouts of depression and self-loathing were coming from. She had asked the Lord — and her superiors — if she could shoulder some of the sufferings of the girls who were wards. Many of the girls who came as wards had been abused or neglected. Some of them had been prostitutes, driven into a life of abuse through poverty. Some of their young spirits were wounded, tormented by guilt, anger, and humiliation.

Once, during Lent, Faustina accepted the depression and suicidal temptations of one of the girls then living in Warsaw. For seven days, she fought against the spirit of despair. Again and again, she had to quench the urge to end her own life. Going about her own duties in the vestiary, Sister Faustina prayed constantly for relief and healing for the girl at risk in Warsaw. And finally, the grace she asked for was given. Mercifully, the urge to kill herself left her — and left the young girl in Warsaw as well.

Perhaps this experience prepared Faustina for the visit from her younger sister, thirteen-year-old Wanda. Wanda had been just a baby when sixteen-year-old Helena had left home in 1921 to go to work. Now she came to see her older sister. She was terribly depressed.

"My sister [Wanda] came to see me," Faustina wrote in her diary a few years later. "When she told me of her plans, I was horror-stricken. How is such a thing possible? Such a beautiful little soul before the Lord, and yet a great darkness had come over her, and she did not know how to help herself. She had a dark view of everything. The good God entrusted her to my care, and for two weeks I was able to work with her. But how many sacrifices this soul cost me is known only to God. For no other soul did I bring so many sacrifices and sufferings and prayers before the throne of God as I did for her soul. I felt that I had forced God to grant her grace. When I reflect on all this, I see that it was truly a miracle. Now I can see how much power intercessory prayer has before God."

Just what Wanda's plans were, Faustina never explained. But Wanda had apparently been desperate for help. For those two weeks, Wanda lived at the convent. Her sister had been given permission to leave her duties to spend all of her time with Wanda or in prayer. Perhaps their parents or oldest, married sister, Josephine Jasinska, had urged Wanda to visit Helena. By now, the family understood that Helena was committed to her vocation in the convent, and that she wouldn't be coming back to them.

On the spring day when Wanda finally headed back to Glogowiec, her eyes were once again young and hopeful. Sister Faustina may have felt as though she had pulled her little sister up a mountain with her own strength and determination. She was exhausted, but so grateful that she dissolved in joyful tears. God was so good. He had saved her little sister, a child she had never really gotten to know.

As soon as Wanda left, her older sister turned her attention to her "other" family. Sister Faustina was to pledge her final vows to her order and to God on May 1, 1933. With the other sisters preparing for vows, she traveled on April 21 to St. Joseph's Convent in Lagiewniki near Cracow.

Like a bride who can hardly wait for her wedding day, Sister Faustina was excited but anxious, bubbling over with joy and love. This final and formal commitment of her life and love to the Lord was quickly approaching. In fact, when a man or woman in religious life takes final vows, the event is like a marriage between a man and a woman. Final vows of poverty, chastity, and obedience are made for life, and they are made out of love — a spousal sort of love for God.

Although Sister Faustina was soon to become "married" to Christ, she was also making a lifelong commitment to the Sisters of Our Lady of Mercy. There were certainly some sisters within the order who didn't think that Faustina fit the congregation. Everyone understood that she had unique gifts. But, when all was said and done, the order accepted Sister Faustina and she said "Yes" to a life with these sisters.

Sister Faustina was so happy that her final vows would be made in Cracow, the place where she had spent her novitiate. In chapel, Jesus reassured her, calming her anxieties about the retreat which was to precede the vows ceremony. Still, nothing had been done about the Divine Mercy image Jesus had asked her to paint. "Be like a child towards him," the Lord told Faustina when she wondered what she should tell her confessor, Father Joseph Andrasz, S.J. She knew that this man would not be her confessor for long.

Forty-two-year-old Father Andrasz had recently been appointed the quarterly confessor for the sisters in the novitiate. In this capacity, he met with the younger sisters preparing for vows only four times a year. Father Andrasz really didn't have any time for an additional commitment. He was edi-

© Marians of the Immaculate Conception

The Reverend Joseph Andrasz, S.J., one of Faustina's confessors.

tor of *Messenger of the Sacred Heart*, a monthly magazine published by the Jesuit publishing house at which he worked. Fortunately for Sister Faustina and the others, however, the time he had to give more than met their needs. He was especially knowledgeable in the fields of pastoral counseling and spirituality. And as Sister Faustina soon discovered, Father Andrasz knew how to listen with his heart.

Mother Mary Joseph Brzoza was also a comforting presence. Sister Faustina was very grateful to have a superior who dealt with her with such charity, such gentleness. When Father Andrasz told Sister Faustina that she should not abandon her mission with the painting, she was surprised. It had been more than two years since Jesus had appeared to her, demanding that she paint His image. She still had doubts about what it all meant.

In a vision, however, she saw Father Sopocko, her future spiritual director, for the second time. She understood that she was to continue to trust that her mission — and Father Sopocko's support of that mission — would unfold and be accomplished in God's time.

Late in the evening of April 30, 1933, Sister Faustina once again lay down to pray on the cold stone floor of the chapel. She pressed her face into her hands, sharing the deepest feelings of her heart with her Lord. On the following day, she was to make her perpetual vows. "My daughter, your heart is My heaven," Jesus told her after she had begged for His mercy.

"Sister Faustina, Sister Faustina, get up!" whispered a sister, reaching down to shake her by the shoulder. Several nuns were preparing to clean and decorate the chapel for the next day's ceremony. "You must go to bed now! It's very late!"

Faustina stood up immediately. Her knees felt very stiff, and she stumbled a bit as she hurried down the hallway. With a smile playing on her pale face, she made her way upstairs to her cell. She slept very little that night. Like a bride on the eve of her wedding, she could only think of the happiness the new day and the new commitment would bring.

On May 1, Sister Mary Faustina and the others in her group lay on the chapel floor underneath a black pall. The pall symbolized a "death to the world" which each sister was now vowing herself to. As Faustina lay beneath the black cloth, she prayed that she would never again offend God with a sin, no matter how small. She also prayed for her congregation, the dying, the souls in purgatory, and her family, who had not been able to come. When Bishop Stanislaus Rospond placed a ring on her finger, God filled her spirit in a profound way. "And since I cannot express that moment, I will be silent about it," she wrote later.

As a perpetually vowed Sister of Our Lady of Mercy, Sister Faustina was soon given a new assignment. On May 25, she boarded a train for Vilnius, where she was to serve as the new gardener. In a way, Faustina regretted being transferred so far away. She loved Cracow and had come to depend on Father Andrasz.

On the way to Vilnius, Sister Faustina and her companion were given permission to make a side trip to visit the shrine of Our Lady of Czestochowa at the Jasna Gora Monastery. Sister Faustina had never been to Czestochowa before, but she knew that it was a beloved shrine to Our Lady in Poland. In 1659, King Jan Kazimierz had proclaimed that the icon of Mary of Czestochowa was the Queen of Poland. In 1656, Swedish armies rolling across Europe were turned back at Jasna Gora, and Poland was saved. Despite later conquests, the Poles never forgot her help and her face. Pilgrims began to visit and pray there.

The little sister from Glogowiec spent six hours in prayer at Czestochowa. She stared up at the unusual "Black Madonna" who cradled her child in her arms, an icon that had been darkened from candles burning nearby over the centuries. Faustina shared her concerns and hopes with the Mother of God. Finally, the two nuns heard the whistle blowing and had to hurry to catch the train headed toward the northwest. They arrived in Vilnius late in the day.

The community at Vilnius was small. "A few scattered tiny huts make up the convent," she wrote of her impressions. "It seems a bit strange to me after the large buildings of Jozefow." Among the eighteen sisters, there were some good friends from earlier years. Sisters Fabiana, Felicia, and Justine hugged Faustina warmly when she arrived. Sister Justine, a friend from the novitiate, had even scrubbed the floor of her friend's cell. It was spotless!

And yet, Sister Faustina was not very comfortable as she began to establish a new routine in this new house. Although she had been moving since she was fifteen, she was now settling into her life as a vowed nun. It was hard to make so many moves. She was the daughter of people who stayed put, who loved their home. Something in her must have longed for a more permanent place to settle herself.

Nonetheless, she soon poured her energies and enthusiasm into her new job as chief gardener. But the back-breaking work of hoeing, digging, and carrying water to irrigate the plants was exhausting. And surprisingly, the former country girl knew very little about vegetable gardening. But this work, too, she accepted willingly and obediently. Often, she weeded with one hand while she held on to her rosary, praying with the other.

Sister Faustina's efforts in the garden were appreciated in her house

— but not by everyone. When Faustina came, Sister Petronela, the sister who had been the gardener, was reassigned to take care of the livestock. The superior thought that gardening would be less taxing for Faustina than some other assignments. Sister Petronela apparently resented being replaced. With mysterious regularity, chickens were found released in the garden, scratching for the seeds which had just been sown. Gardening tools disappeared.

The new gardener endured this rash of "misfortunes" bravely. Then she enlisted the help of a missionary brother who was stationed nearby. He had been a professional gardener and Faustina quickly learned more than enough. She started her own greenhouse and the convent gardens were soon prospering.

But in other areas of her life, she held back. She really didn't want to bare her soul immediately to Father Michael Sopocko, the newly appointed convent confessor. Faustina knew that the forty-four-year-old Vilnius native was an exceptionally gifted priest. She also knew that Jesus had selected this man as her spiritual director. Faustina knew this because she twice had seen him in a vision! She smiled in church on the day that she first saw him in person. Very quickly, she went to confession. Carefully and in a reserved but detailed way, she explained to him that God had shown him to her as her future spiritual director.

Father Sopocko listened respectfully. Sister Faustina, he could immediately see, was a deeply religious woman. She was intelligent and courageous. But he was also a very busy man. He didn't have time immediately to dwell on her case. In addition to his job as confessor for the sisters, he was also a theology professor at the seminary and at Stefan Batory University. And he was pastor at St. Michael's Church in Vilnius.

© Marians of the Immaculate Conception

Father Sopocko had extensive experience as a spiritual director. He had been an army chaplain during the First World War, then spiritual director for the diocesan seminary in Vilnius. Father Sopocko's field of academic expertise was pastoral theology. He knew how well-intentioned people could be deluded and confused. He decided to test Faustina's messages and he questioned the authenticity of her reports.

The Reverend Michael Sopocko, confessor and spiritual director for Faustina. His own beatification process was begun in 1987.

Sister Faustina recoiled against

such treatment. Still regretting the loss of her understanding confessor, Father Andrasz, she quickly began to withhold her deeper concerns. She believed in absolute obedience to her Lord, but she didn't always live it out. Within a few weeks, her confessions became superficial and perfunctory, and she temporarily sought out another confessor, a Jesuit named Dabrowski. At the same time, the troubled sister also knew that the Lord wasn't pleased with the way that she was shutting out Father Sopocko.

Father Dabrowski also insisted on testing this nun who was telling him such fantastic things. Hemmed in at every turn, Faustina soon returned to Father Sopocko. She told him in confession that she was ready to accept any test he felt was necessary. She also told him the complete story of her visions and her commission from Jesus. Immediately, she was blessed by her confession. "Now I understand what it means to be faithful to a particular grace," she later wrote. "That one grace draws down a whole series of others."

It continued to seem to Sister Faustina, that spiritual progress was coming only through adversity. In October, during a Holy Hour, Sister Faustina struggled to focus on prayer. But she couldn't hold any prayerful thoughts in her mind. After more than two hours, she decided to kneel on the chapel floor with outstretched arms. Soon, her body ached for rest. Faustina pulled the ring from her finger and reminded Jesus that it was a symbol of their unity.

At that moment, she was filled with a sense of God's love. Jesus appeared. At first, He looked glorious and joyful, exactly as He looked on the day of her perpetual vows. Then, just as quickly, He was stripped of his clothes and covered with blood. His eyes were glassy with tears and He murmured to her, "The bride must resemble the bridegroom."

The sister humbly lowered her arms and bowed her head. She understood. She would be like Jesus when she was suffering.

By fall, Father Sopocko's attitude had also changed. Faced with the full story of her visions and messages, he had begun to believe in her. To test his own conclusions, however, he went to Sister Faustina's superior. He asked about the psychological health of Sister Mary Faustina. "Is she prone to exaggeration?" "Does Sister Faustina have difficulties seeing reality?" Did the slender nun in charge of the garden relate well to others — or was she a recluse, an unhappy misfit? The confessor needed to know.

Mother Irene Krzyzanowska, the superior of the house at Vilnius, defended Sister Faustina as a balanced, well-adjusted woman. Though many of her fellow sisters did not understand her, Faustina was always well-liked. People were attracted to her natural goodness, to her outgoing and friendly style of relating. She had a sense of humor. Faustina seemed to love life as well as the Lord with great intensity.

But still, Father Sopocko was not sure. He asked that Sister Faustina be given a complete physical and psychological examination.

Dr. Helena Maciejewska, a psychiatrist and the physician for the convent, examined Sister Faustina. She found her patient exceptionally well-balanced and psychologically healthy in every way. If Sister Faustina resented being placed under the microscope and cross-examined from every perspective, she didn't show it. Slowly, a deep trust and honesty grew between her and her spiritual director.

Sister Faustina realized Father Sopocko's great gifts, and listened to his counsels. He told her to rejoice in the humiliations she suffered on behalf of the Lord and her mission. And "be patient," he advised her. "True works of God always meet with opposition and are marked by suffering. If God wants to accomplish something, sooner or later He will do so in spite of the difficulties."

And soon, something was accomplished! Right after the New Year, Father Sopocko told Sister Faustina that she was to visit a painter he knew. He was Eugene Kazimierowski, a professor at the university and a friend of Father Sopocko's. Kazimierowski also lived fairly near the convent.

Father Sopocko spoke with the artist and asked him to work with Sister Faustina to reproduce the image she'd seen in a vision. On January 2, 1934, Sister Faustina rose even earlier than usual. She was excited about the short trip she was to take into Vilnius with Mother Irene. On that day, she met with the artist for the first time. At Father Sopocko's direction, she later met with him every week to direct the painting.

So that the other sisters would not question her about her unique experiences, the weekly visits were camouflaged, according to Mother Irene. For a while, Mother Irene herself accompanied Faustina to see the painter. Each Saturday morning, she reported, "I went with her to Holy Mass at the Ostra Brama Gate, and after Mass we would go to the painter, to whom Sister Faustina would give exact details as to how he was to paint the picture of the Merciful Jesus." After a while, however, Mother Irene appointed Sister Borgia Tichy, a discreet forty-seven-year-old nurse, to accompany Faustina.

As the painting developed, Faustina's spiritual director told her to ask Jesus about the meaning of the rays in the image. Understanding what they meant would help the painter to do his job. Sister Faustina prayed, asking Jesus what the rays meant. Soon, the answer came.

"The two rays denote Blood and Water," Jesus answered. "The pale ray stands for the Water which makes souls righteous. The red ray stands for the Blood which is the life of souls. These two rays issued forth from the very depth of My tender mercy when My agonized Heart was opened by a lance on the Cross."

This answer moved Father Michael Sopocko profoundly when he stared one morning at the unfinished painting in his friend's studio. The rays, he saw, symbolized the sacraments. In particular, the pale rays symbolized baptism; the red, the Eucharist. The life of God was mercifully given to the world through these sacraments. He shook his head in awe and in humility. He was gradually realizing what an extraordinary and blessed woman Sister Mary Faustina really was. And he was coming to understand that the messages she was being given by God really were meant for the world.

But the responsibility for Sister Faustina's spiritual direction began to weigh heavily upon Father Sopocko. He was terribly busy as a theology professor, pastor, and chaplain. Added to that, he was also preparing work for his own post-doctoral research. In order to conscientiously deal with Sister Faustina, he asked her to begin writing a diary.

As he later explained, "So that Sister Faustina's confessions should not become too long, I asked her at confession to accuse herself of her sins only, and if she had anything else to say, to write it and give it to me to read."

Father Sopocko's request of Sister Faustina couldn't have been more inspired. Though neither of them could have imagined it, the suggestion he'd made to save time in the confessional was to have profound and evangelical fruit for the world one day. Like a mustard seed, the diary began in a very small and unpretentious way.

On the evening of July 28, 1934, a tired twenty-eight-year-old Sister Faustina lit the little oil lamp on her desk in her small cell. She pulled out the chair and sat down. She opened a ledger-style ruled notebook which measured about six-and-one-half inches by eight inches. Mother Irene had given her the notebook and a fountain pen. Instinctively, she put a small cross in the upper left corner above "J.M.J," the initials for "Jesus, Mary, Joseph." After a few seconds, she began to write:

"I am to write down the encounters of my soul with You, O God, at the moments of Your special visitations. I am to write about You, O Incomprehensible in mercy towards my poor soul. Your holy will is the life of my soul."

After leaning over her notebook for a half-hour or more, the sister couldn't stop yawning. It was hot and the day had been a tiring one. Fatigue was battling her will. Shaking her weary head a bit to ward off sleepiness, Sister Faustina reread the first entry of her diary. It did not seem to say half of what she wanted to say. But she flipped the notebook shut, recapped her pen, and put pen and notebook back into the desk drawer.

The young woman was exhausted as she removed her veil and habit and slipped into her nightgown. Her back and knees ached from hoeing that day in the garden. But for a few minutes, she dropped to her knees again beside her bed. "Good night, Jesus," she whispered finally and got into bed.

10

Days of Work, Struggle, and Suffering

Every morning, I prepare myself for the whole day's struggle.
Holy Communion assures me that I will win the victory; and
so it is. . . . The Bread of the Strong gives me all the strength I
need to carry on my mission and the courage to do whatever
the Lord asks of me — **Diary, 91**.

During almost all of the hot, sticky July days of 1934, Sister Faustina had been extremely weary. In her newly initiated diary, she had ominously noted that "Days of work, of struggle and suffering have begun."

There had been too much rain in Vilnius! The convent gardener had had to wield her hoe like the sword of an avenging angel. Weeds threatened to overrun her beans, potatoes, spinach, beets, cabbage, and carrots. And each large crop of vegetables, after all, was that many more bowls of good soup for the convent tables.

But, there were other reasons why the young nun seemed a bit sluggish, a bit wearier than usual. There were certain disappointments and difficulties that Sister Faustina was trying to graciously and privately accept. And the strain to do so added to the usual gardener complaints — aches in the back, shoulders, and legs.

The first and hardest cross of the summer had come in June. Every Saturday morning throughout late winter and spring, Faustina and Sister Borgia had gone secretly to Vilnius to consult with Professor Eugene Kazimierowski, the artist who was carrying out the Lord's command to "paint an image." The problem, of course, was that Jesus said to create the image "According to the pattern *you* see." Kazimierowski had never seen the image. He depended upon the memory and the descriptive powers of the young nun who was the gardener.

By June, however, the artist considered his job done. When Faustina realized that, she could scarcely conceal her crushing disappointment. Perhaps she had thought that Kazimierowski would paint until the painting reproduced the glorious vision she had seen. He did not. And on that June day when he told her that the painting was completed, she traveled home from Vilnius, barely holding back the tears. Later in the day, she went to the chapel where she cried and cried. "Who will paint You as beautiful as You are?" she wailed to Jesus.

Jesus had answered immediately. "Not in the beauty of the color nor of the brush lies the greatness of this image, but in My grace." The painting was simply a visual symbol of Christ's endless love. The world needed to be reminded of that love, and even the flawed image painted by Professor Kazimierowski served well enough as a reminder. In fact, Sister Faustina soon accepted the painting in just those terms. It was not what Jesus looked like. But — it was the visible reminder of His mercy. Even though she understood that, she may have been relieved that the painting was not hanging in her own convent. Father Sopocko had taken it. He had it hung in a corridor of the convent of the Bernardine Sisters near the church of St. Michael in Vilnius, where he was pastor.

But there were other special burdens in Faustina's new life at Vilnius. Soon after she had begun to keep the diary, some of the sisters began to grumble about her "scribblings." Sister Faustina was a nun of the second choir. It was really not her vocation to dwell on matters that required intellectual reflection or scholarship. "Doesn't she have enough to do?" the sisters indignantly complained to the superior.

Mother Irene knew that Faustina's "scribbling"wasn't whimsical. It was a matter of obedience — obedience to her confessor. But the superior was guarded in her replies, and she really could not spare Sister Faustina from all the criticisms. Mother Irene had wisely assigned her to the gardens to give her more freedom of movement. Actually, Faustina had become an excellent cook and could have better served the house in the kitchen.

The sister-gardener felt many eyes following her. Sometimes, the eyes felt like daggers — ready to stab or jab. In many ways, the insinuations and the misunderstandings had become more severe here in Vilnius than at any other convent where Faustina had lived. There were just eighteen sisters at Vilnius, but several of them disliked Faustina. In such a small community, all the nuns knew who ate too much and who smiled too long at the deliverymen. In this setting, there was little room for secrets.

Despite the climate of criticism, Sister Faustina was still trying to keep her diary. She now felt a commitment to it. She grabbed a few minutes here and there during the day to write. She wrote at night when she could snatch some time. But putting down her thoughts and her conversations with Jesus had become much more complicated. And there was a reason for that, too.

While Father Sopocko was in Palestine for several months during the first half of 1934, Sister Faustina was without her trusted confessor. One night, she had a vision. A young man appeared. He told her that her diary was useless and would only cause anxieties. "Throw it into the fire," the young man ordered. She did so.

When her confessor returned and learned that Sister Faustina had indeed burned her diary of Christ's messages, he was very upset. He told his penitent that she had been misled by an evil apparition. "Reconstruct what you have destroyed," he told her. So, when she began to write the diary again, she had to record any messages and inspirations she'd received that day. But, she was also told to go back and rewrite what had been written months earlier. Though she intended to do it, she never quite found the time to rewrite all of those lost portions of her diary. Some of it — especially the memories of her early life and childhood — was never fully reconstructed.

Four months had elapsed since Jesus had asked Sister Faustina to offer herself in a new way for sinners — especially those who had lost hope in His mercy. After consulting with Father Sopocko, she had agreed to do it. Soon, she found what this new ministry meant. In her diary she wrote that she soon experienced "all the sufferings, fears and terrors with which sinners are filled. In return, I give them all the consolations which my soul receives from my communion with God."

What a gift Sister Faustina was giving! But what a sacrifice she was making to give the gift. Sometimes, it was all she could do to keep from shouting the blasphemies and curses that seethed within sinners. At other times, she raked or hoed in the rows of onions and cabbages with a quiet smile on her face. But inside her, feelings of distrust or despair, accepted from another person's spirit, weighed her down.

One hot July day, something new happened out in the garden. Sister Faustina was working happily with the girls assigned to assist her. Suddenly, her guardian angel said, "Pray for the dying."

Sister Faustina said immediately, "Girls, let's pray a rosary right now for the dying. They need our prayers so much. We can pray while we finish the weeding and watering." When the rosary and a few other prayers were completed, Faustina heard a different voice. It was the voice of a sister in Warsaw. "Pray for me," the voice pleaded. "Pray for me until I tell you to stop. I am dying."

Sister Faustina prayed intensely from three until about five p.m. Then, she heard the sister's voice say, "Thank you!" The next day, a postcard arrived from Warsaw with the news that Sister Philomena Andrejko had died the day before at 4:45 p.m. It was the first of many occasions in which Faustina interceded with great devotion and persistence for a person who was dying. Sometimes, Faustina knew the person; sometimes she didn't. It didn't matter. She knew that she was helping to escort some man or woman into the loving arms of God.

In mid-summer, Mary, the Mother of Jesus, appeared to Sister Faustina. The Blessed Virgin gently warned the sister that she would soon become very ill. She also predicted that the doctors would complicate rather than aid her recovery.

In the last week of July, Sister Faustina came down with what seemed to be a cold. Nobody thought much of that. The Vilnius buildings were cool at night. And the dank summer weather could easily be blamed for the chills and fever which soon accompanied her cough.

On Thursday evening, August 9, Sister Faustina walked outside to the chapel building just before eleven p.m. Each Thursday, the Sisters kept a Holy Hour from nine to ten p.m. But on this Thursday, adoration in front of the Blessed Sacrament had been scheduled all night long. During her prayer, the gardener didn't worry about the rabbits nibbling on her carrots in the moonlight. She generously interceded for sinners.

At the end of her Holy Hour, when Jesus told Sister Faustina how pleased He was with her prayers of atonement, she was very happy. "The prayer of a humble and loving soul disarms the anger of My Father and draws down an ocean of blessings," He said.

It was after midnight when Sister Faustina pulled her shawl tightly around her to protect her throat and chest against the cool night air. She left the chapel, pulling the door shut behind her. Then she turned to walk the dirt path back to the dormitory building. Out of the bushes and dark shadows sprang a pack of huge, black dogs. The dogs were jumping and snapping at her. Terrified, she froze and stood still. Her heart began to race and she wondered if her sisters would hear her if she screamed for help. Then one of the dogs spoke. Sister Faustina quickly understood that these beasts were not really dogs.

"Because you have snatched so many souls away from us this night, we will tear you to pieces," snarled a raspy voice which came from a dog in the middle of the pack.

Faustina's courage had returned and she boldly told the demon, "If that is the will of the most merciful God, tear me to pieces, for I have justly deserved it, because I am the most miserable of all sinners, and God is ever holy, just and infinitely merciful."

With that, the demon-dogs ran from her. "Let us flee, for she is not alone," another dog had howled. "The Almighty is with her!" Sister Faustina, quickening her pace, headed for bed and began to hum the "*Te Deum*."

Three days later, on Sunday, August 12, Sister Faustina could not rise from her bed. It was, as she later reported in her diary, a foretaste of death.

"Suddenly, I felt sick, I gasped for breath, there was darkness before my eyes, my limbs grew numb — and there was a terrible suffocation. Even a moment of such suffocation is extremely long. There also comes a strange fear, in spite of trust. I wanted to receive the last sacraments, but it was extremely difficult to make a confession even though I desired to do so. A person does not know what he is saying; not finishing one thing, he begins another."

Father Sopocko was called and came immediately. Sadly, he administered the Anointing of the Sick to the remarkable young woman he'd come to know so recently. Right away, there was relief in the patient's labored breathing and in her color. But about an hour after that, she suffered a second attack. Again, she thought that she was dying. However, the attack was not so severe as the first one. Doctors had given Sister Faustina some medications to alleviate her agonies.

As the young sister revived a bit, she awoke to see black figures swarming around her room. They showed their hatred and loathing for her and one of them said, "Be damned, you and He who is within you, for you are beginning to torment us even in hell." When Faustina weakly muttered a reference to the Word made flesh, the demons disappeared.

Within a few days, a very weak Sister Faustina managed to walk to the chapel for Mass. "Jesus, I thought You were going to take me," she told her Lord. Jesus said that she would not remain on earth much longer. He also told her that He wanted her to grow in selfless surrender for sinners so that her last moments of life could resemble His.

Though Sister Faustina had almost died, some of the other sisters didn't wait long to resume their heckling. She was too secretive, too proud of her own spiritual gifts, too ready to drop her assigned work — too "different"!

Sister Faustina remained silent, clinging to one thing only for support. In her diary, she noted, "Every morning, I prepare myself for the whole day's struggle. Holy Communion assures me that I will win the victory; and so it is. . . . The Bread of the Strong gives me all the strength I need to carry on my mission and the courage to do whatever the Lord asks of me."

Within a few weeks, autumn was washing the woods around Vilnius with reds and golds. Sister Faustina was working hard to harvest her vegetables. It was gratifying work for a farmer's daughter. Many of the vegetables were stored in root cellars or dried by the convent cook and her assistants. Sister Faustina, a self-taught gardener, was also pleased with her first flower gardens. The gardens had produced beautifully. She was happy with the bright, beautiful blossoms that could be cut each day for the chapel altar.

On Friday, October 26, Sister Faustina and some of the students were leaving the garden to come in for supper at ten minutes before six. Suddenly, above the chapel, Faustina saw Jesus of the Divine Mercy. He appeared just as He had in 1931. The rays which came out of his heart progressively spread out over the convent grounds and over the city beyond the gates. The vision lasted about four minutes. Sister Faustina stood and watched, trying to conceal the joy and excitement she felt. The girls who worked for her were laughing and walking ahead of her.

However, one girl, Imelda, had been walking side by side with Sister Faustina. She too stopped and stared at the sky. When it was over, she shouted to the other girls about the strange and beautiful rays of light she had seen. Faustina could see that she had seen the rays, but not Jesus. When Imelda later approached Faustina about the phenomenon, the nun could only shrug her shoulders in feigned ignorance.

About a week later, on November 5, Sister Faustina stopped into the chapel to share an idea with her Lord. She told Him that she wished to dedicate the day's work, sufferings, mortifications, and prayers for the intentions of the Holy Father so that he might establish the Feast of Mercy. Jesus encouraged her. He told her to make a novena for this intention, using the prayer He had already given her: "O Blood and Water which gushed forth from the Heart of Jesus as a fount of mercy for us, I trust in you."

More and more, Sister Faustina was recognizing that the Divine Mercy image, the mercy prayers she was receiving, and the Feast of Mercy were all God's gifts to the suffering world. She knew that she was not to hoard these gifts. Neither was she to permit them to be hidden or discarded. She could see that Jesus wanted her to proclaim the "Good News" about God's mercy as far as her voice would carry.

During the seasons of Advent and Christmas, the convent gardener often had visions of the Child Jesus. She was struck by that and questioned the Lord about it. Why was He appearing to her so often as a little child? she asked Him.

"I commune only with those who are little. I demand of you a childlike spirit," He answered. Jesus appeared as a tiny infant up on the altar during the Christmas Eve Midnight Mass. Faustina's heart was overjoyed. She smiled as she saw Him stretch out His arms and gaze at everyone.

As the new year of 1935 began, there were changes in the Vilnius convent. Mother Borgia Tichy became superior. She was the sister who had accompanied Sister Faustina on so many trips to see the artist while the Divine Mercy image was being painted. Mother Borgia was well-suited to guide the small community, which included a twenty-nine-year-old gardener with an extraordinary mission for the world. She believed in Sister Faustina and her spiritual gifts.

At the end of January, Faustina had an inner vision about the Holy Father, Pope Pius XI. More and more frequently, she was receiving such visions about events that were taking place simultaneously. At that moment, the Holy Father was saying Mass. During a period of meditation after the "Our Father," he sat down and was considering something that was crucial to Sister Faustina's mission. It was the establishment of the Feast of Divine Mercy.

Faustina's vision was corroborated later by Father Sopocko. While in Rome at that time, he had gone to the Vatican to present and discuss the idea of the Feast of Divine Mercy. Although he wasn't able to meet with the pope, Father Sopocko did consult with the Papal Nuncio, Archbishop Cortesim. The archbishop had apparently discussed it with the pope.

On February 4, Sister Faustina and others began an eight-day retreat. After the first conference, Jesus told her that a new phase of her spiritual life would soon begin. Referring to her daily habit of recording her spiritual goals, He told her: "Write these words on a clean sheet of paper: 'From today on, my own will does not exist,' and then cross out the page. And on the other side write these words: 'From today on, I do the Will of God everywhere, always and in everything.'"

An awesome goal. An unthinkable and unreasonable project to most human beings! But Sister Mary Faustina immediately took the eradication of her own will most seriously. On February 8, in her diary entry, she methodically listed the four parts to this cancellation of her own personal will. It would involve, she reasoned, the denial of "my reason," "my will," "my judgment," and "my tongue." These denials could be accomplished through subjecting herself through obedience "to those who represent God to me here on earth." By those who represented God, the sister meant her spiritual director and her superiors.

Shortly after the retreat was over, Faustina had a poignant experience of what it meant to deny her will and judgment. A letter from Glogowiec arrived. It was handed to her by Mother Borgia, who had already read it.

In the letter, Sister Faustina learned that her mother, who was almost sixty, was deathly ill and asking to see Helena "one last time." Sister Faustina wept when she read the news. Her weeping brought a nostalgia and longing for the home and family she'd left so many years before. When she'd reread the letter, she folded it and replaced it in the envelope. Then, she went to the chapel and prayed for her mother. But, in her prayer, Sister Faustina knew that the decision to honor her mother's wish was no longer up to her. She later slipped the letter into her desk drawer and waited to see what God's will would be. After all, she had canceled out her own will with the slash of a pen.

On Friday, February 15, Mother Borgia gave Sister Faustina a second letter from Glogowiec. Her family was begging her to come home. Mother Borgia gave her permission to leave and Faustina went to pack. She left Vilnius that evening and traveled southwest to Warsaw and then further towards Lodz. It was a journey of about two hundred fifty miles.

Finally, at about eight on the following evening — Saturday night — Sister Faustina stepped out of a taxi, grabbed her small suitcase, and walked in the dark up the snowy road to the brick cottage where she'd been born. She saw golden squares of light shining out the windows on soft shoulders of snow near the picket fence. Over in the barn, she could hear one of her father's cows lowing softly. Her heart was pounding with mixed emotions as she walked around the house to the courtyard and knocked with her gloved knuckles on the wooden door.

Was her mother still alive? If she was, would she recognize her? Did her

© Marians of the Immaculate Conception

Faustina during the visit she made home to her family. Her parents are on the right; her godparents on the left.

family still harbor resentments for her choice of religious life, a life which kept her away from them so much? What would it be like to be in this house again? It was the house of her childhood, the place where she first realized that she belonged to the Lord.

"Helena!" Sister Faustina's little sister Wanda, now fifteen years old, greeted her with an emotional embrace. The youngster pulled her quickly into the warm room and took her sister's bag. Faustina could see that there was peace and joy in her little sister's eyes. And she'd grown so much taller — and prettier — in the two years since she'd seen her.

"Papa, Papa! Everyone! Look who's here! It's Helena!" Wanda cried out.

Near the fireplace, Sister Faustina saw her father rise slowly from his chair and turn towards her. He was sixty-six, and the years of hard, grueling work as a carpenter and farmer had taken their toll. "Papa," she said, smiling, going to her father. "Praised be Jesus Christ."

Stanislaus put his heavy, scarred hands upon her shoulders to study the face of his third daughter — the daughter he cherished so much. A warm smile wreathed his wrinkled face, lifting the ends of his mustache, which was now peppered with gray.

"You are too thin, daughter," he whispered, looking down at her, "But still so lovely! My beautiful Helena!"

Sister Faustina smiled and then followed her gathering family to her mother's bed. "Praised be Jesus Christ," she said, kneeling by her bed and taking her mother's hand. As Marianna's eyes found the face of her Helena, they brightened with excitement and joy. Within a few seconds, the sick woman's face was suddenly less pale, less drawn with pain. Faustina sensed that Jesus would allow her mother to revive in order to enjoy this rare visit.

"Mother, you will be up and about yet. I want to talk with you," Sister Faustina told her mother cheerfully. When Marianna sat up, smiling broadly, another daughter who was standing near the stove in another area of the small house called out, "Mother, are you well already?"

"Yes," Marianna replied, "As soon as I saw her, I got well."

Marianna did indeed get up. In fact, she recovered from her illness and outlived Helena by many years. But on this Saturday evening in February 1935, she knew that this special daughter was home again. In fact, in the next few days, when word of Sister Faustina's visit spread through the neighborhood of Glogowiec, almost all of the Kowalski children — and some grandchildren — gathered again in the roadside Kowalski cottage. Everyone clustered around the "celebrity." They wanted to talk with her, listen to her, show off their children to her. The mothers of little ones put their infants and toddlers into her arms, begging her to hold, bless, and kiss the babies.

Helena rejoiced that she was able to spend time with her family again. This was the home she remembered, and yet. . . . "O how everything had changed beyond recognition during those ten years!" she wrote later in her diary. "The garden had been so small, and now I could not recognize it. My brothers and sisters had still been children, and now they were all grown up. I was surprised that I did not find them as they had been when we parted."

Soon, she found that the non-stop visiting at home was exhausting. Besides that, there was almost no time to pray, to communicate with her Lord.

"I struck on one way of getting some respite," she wrote in her diary later. "I asked my brothers to sing for me, inasmuch as they had lovely voices; and besides, one played the violin; another, the mandolin. And during this time I was able to devote myself to interior prayer without shunning their company."

Her brother Stanley accompanied Sister Faustina to Mass each day at the parish church at Swinice. She realized that her brother was very pleasing to God. It was so easy to talk with him about God. And it was so wonderful to pray again at St. Casimir's. Faustina quickly realized that God had richly blessed her. He'd given her such devout and prayerful parents and home-life. But all too soon, the time came to leave. Sister Faustina had to return to Vilnius, and everyone in the family sensed that she would never be home again. It was very hard.

Faustina and her extended family, also taken during her visit home.

"Although everyone was crying," she noted in her diary, "I did not shed a single tear. I tried to be brave and comforted them as best I could, reminding them of heaven where there would be no more parting.

"Stanley walked with me to the car. I told him how much God loves pure souls and assured him that God was satisfied with him. When I was telling him about the goodness of God and of how He thinks of us, he burst out crying like a little child, and I was not surprised for his was a pure soul and, as such, more capable of recognizing God.

"Once I was in the car, I let my heart have its way and I, too, cried like a baby, for joy that God was granting our family so many graces, and I became steeped in a prayer of thanksgiving."

That evening, a tired Sister Faustina was back in Warsaw. As the car pulled up in front of the convent on Zytnia Street, she got out, picked up her suitcase, realizing how happy she was to arrive at this "home." She went, first of all, to the chapel, to "the Lord of the house" to pray. The next day, Mother Superior Mary Joseph Brzoza took her to see Mother General Michael Moraczewska, who had accepted the twenty-nine-year-old Sister Faustina into the congregation as a teenager.

The next day, Sister Mary Faustina, the convent gardener, was back in her convent at Vilnius. Fatigued from her travels and the emotional experiences at home, she was nonetheless full of joy. The visit to her family had been wonderful, but she had changed so much. She was not really the same Helena that they remembered. And she could see that some of the members of her family still did not fully accept that she belonged to another household, another family now.

"I felt as though I were entering the convent a second time,"she reported in her diary that night. "I took unending delight in the silence and peace in which the soul can so easily immerse itself in God, helped by everyone and disturbed by no one."

Mother Michael Moraczewska, superior of the house in Warsaw and later Superior General of the Congregation.

Sister Mary Joseph Brzoza, directress of Faustina's novitiate class.

11

Plans for a New Congregation

*O my God, I am conscious of my mission in the Holy Church. It is my constant endeavor to plead for mercy for the world. I unite myself closely with Jesus and stand before Him as an atoning sacrifice on behalf of the world. God will refuse me nothing when I entreat Him with the voice of His Son — **Diary, 482**.*

As spring began to warm and soften the cold earth of Vilnius, the convent's gardener prepared to plant the first crops of the year. Peas, beets, carrots, and lettuce. Those were on the list, first of all. But the hoeing had to be done before the seeds could be planted, and Sister Faustina and the girls who worked with her were cheerfully at work when March arrived.

Jesus also seemed to be preparing Faustina's soul as though it were a garden where good things would grow. During Lent, as she meditated on the Lord's Passion with increasing frequency, she seemed to come closer and closer to the Lord. Often, during these meditations, she had visions of the suffering Christ. Once, she saw Jesus being crowned with the crown of thorns, just after the scourging.

Jesus, she wrote in her diary, was forced to sit on a beam. He was being made fun of, taunted, slapped, and hit by the men's fists. "Who can comprehend Him — comprehend His suffering? Jesus' eyes were downcast. I sensed what was happening in the most sweet Heart of Jesus at that time. Let every soul reflect on what Jesus was suffering at that moment."

This unity with Jesus, with God and His whole heaven, was deepening in the young woman's life. She was maturing beyond her twenty-nine years. In the spiritual dimension, she was profoundly in tune with her Creator and His loving, merciful relationship with the world. During Mass, she saw God within her soul and felt the Divine Presence permeate her entire being.

She understood more and more — and loved God more and more. She had many moments of spiritual ecstasy, though few of the sisters or girls she lived with would have guessed it.

But there was a frightening side to Sister Faustina's holiness. Devils began to threaten her with increasing frequency. Often, they appeared as hideous beasts. One day, when she was in the chapel, Satan hurled a flower pot and smashed it on the floor. That same evening, she awoke to find her bed shaking. When she began to pray to her guardian angel for protection, she saw purgatory with tormented souls. One of these devils, transformed into a cat, jumped onto her bed and lay on her feet. He was so heavy that she couldn't cast him off. So she bravely began to pray the Rosary. After several hours, the spirits disappeared and Faustina fell asleep.

The frosty days of March melted, and Holy Week began. Sister Faustina prepared to unite herself with the suffering Redeemer. On Holy Thursday, April 18, Jesus told Sister Faustina that she wouldn't sense His presence in her soul again until the Mass on Easter morning. This was an agonizing deprivation, and the separation she felt from Jesus ripped her heart apart. At Communion time, she saw the face of the tortured Christ in the hosts in the ciborium. An even greater feeling of longing flooded her as she knelt quietly in her pew.

At three o'clock on Good Friday, Sister Faustina entered the chapel. It was the hour in which the Church traditionally commemorated the death of Jesus on the cross. Just as she crossed the threshold, she heard the words of the Lord: "I desire that the image be publicly honored." Then she experienced a vision of Christ, gasping in pain, close to death. The rays of light suddenly came forth from His chest, spreading out to the world. These rays were just like the rays in the Divine Mercy image which Jesus was asking to be displayed. In a sense, Jesus had asked for this public honor with His last breaths.

Within a few days, Sister Faustina arranged to see her spiritual director, Father Sopocko, in the convent parlor. "Father," she said, "on Good Friday, Jesus said, 'I desire that the image be publicly honored.' " Sister Faustina then suggested that the image should be displayed for three days at the church at Our Lady of Mercy in the Dawn Gate (also called the *Ostra Brama* or *Eastern Gate*). As Sister and Father both knew very well, a celebration was already planned at Ostra Brama to mark the end of the Jubilee Year of the Redemption. The closing ceremonies of that celebration had already been scheduled for April 26 to 28. That was a week away!

"That can't be done!" responded Father Sopocko at first. It was just not possible to add a new devotion to ceremonies which had probably been planned months earlier. And even if the celebrations hadn't been finalized, what influence could a university professor have in the matter?

But the priest saw from Faustina's gray-green eyes that she could not accept "no" for an answer. He knew her *very* well. She was unfailingly obedient and respectful of his authority as her spiritual director. But this was a different matter.

The forty-six-year-old priest stroked his chin and shut his eyes to focus on the problem. What should he do? As he considered the words Jesus had spoken to Faustina, it struck him. April 28 was the day that the Jubilee Year ended. But it was also Mercy Sunday, the Sunday after Easter!

"I will try to talk to the archbishop," Father Sopocko said finally. Sister Faustina's smile was one of pure joy. With an inner knowledge that she was often given, she could already foresee that the archbishop would finally agree. The Divine Mercy image would be displayed just as Jesus wanted it, just as Jesus had planned it — on the Sunday after Easter, on April 28!

On Thursday, April 25, the image was carefully hoisted and mounted in a window in the Ostra Brama church. It was hung high so that many people could see it. Thousands of people were expected to attend the ceremonies closing the Jubilee Year. Displaying the painting by Kazimierowski at the Jubilee ceremonies would bring the Divine Mercy image to the attention of massive crowds.

Sister Faustina and Mother Borgia went in to Vilnius to see Father Sopocko. The two sisters wondered if anything else needed to be done. Arrangements to display the image had been hastily made. When Father Sopocko asked if the sisters could make some wreaths to decorate the church, Mother Superior quickly responded, "Sister Faustina will help."

Sister Faustina was elated to be "volunteered." And it was natural that the convent's head gardener would oversee the cutting of greens and flowers for wreaths. But the project soon brought her pain and embarrassment. When several Vilnius ladies saw the beautiful but mysterious image of Jesus in the church on Thursday, they were very curious. On Friday, April 16, they asked other Sisters of Our Lady of Mercy about the picture of Jesus.

"What picture?" the sisters answered. When they learned that the convent gardener — Sister Faustina — had been seen at church decorating the painting, they were deeply embarrassed. Where did the picture come from? Why didn't *all* the sisters of the house know about it? Why was a second-choir sister spending her time on such matters? Didn't she have some hoeing to do in the pea patch?

Sister Faustina didn't confront the blunt questions or complaints of some of her fellow sisters. Her superiors knew why. Discussing the Divine Mercy image seemed to be unwise because she would have to present herself as the visionary — the sister whom God had favored in a special way. Sister Faustina didn't believe that she was any better, any holier, than her sisters. But admitting that heaven had given her such a lofty mission was hard to do gracefully.

Instead of explaining, she waited for the chatter about the mysterious Divine Mercy image to run dry. In the meantime, she — and the other sisters of the house — attended the ceremonies at the Dawn Gate on Friday, Saturday, and Sunday.

On Friday, she sat in church with the other nuns and listened as Father Sopocko preached a sermon on the Divine Mercy of Jesus. Inside her heart, there was a profound peace and joy. To hear the good news of the Savior's loving mercy presented in such an appealing new way was glorious.

To look and see the Divine Mercy image hanging high on the church wall for thousands to see — that too was so wonderful! From time to time, Faustina's eyes were brimming with happy tears. But thousands of other eyes were trained on the same image. Without hearing detailed explanations of the rays which flowed from the Savior's chest, people instantly sensed that life and love were

© Marians of the Immaculate Conception

Jesus I Trust In You! ©

The first image of The Divine Mercy, painted by E. Kazimierowski in 1934.

flowing out toward them. There was something very comforting and attractive about this new painting of Jesus, hung so high up on the church wall.

Before the end of Friday's service, Sister Faustina got up and slipped out of church to return to the convent. Perhaps she had duties that beckoned her back early. Perhaps she merely wanted to avoid questions about the Divine Mercy image from some of the townspeople. Just as she left the church and began walking down the street, many demons confronted her. They had come, they admitted, from human hearts. "Stop tormenting us," they shrieked at her.

Though frightened, the slender sister appealed for protection from her guardian angel. Strong and peaceful, the angel appeared and assured her that no harm would come to her. And then, he accompanied her back to the convent doorstep. As Sister Faustina noted, he remained visable to her. "A flame of fire sparkled from his forehead," she noted in her diary.

On Sunday, April 28, Sister Faustina was sitting again in the beautiful Ostra Brama Church. She saw Jesus of the Divine Mercy blessing the whole world. Then, she saw a vision of the Trinity — a crystal dwelling with three doors. After Jesus entered one of the doors, Sister Faustina heard His voice saying: "This Feast emerged from the very depths of My mercy, and it is confirmed in the vast depths of My tender mercies. Every soul believing and trusting in My mercy will obtain it."

After the celebrations marking the end of the Jubilee Year, the Divine Mercy image painted by Professor Kazimierowski was returned to a dark convent-corridor of the Bernardine sisters. But Sister Faustina realized that the image was to be hidden only for a short time. The people of Vilnius had seen and loved it. A powerful and loving devotion to the Divine Mercy would have to wait a bit longer to emerge. But it was there, waiting to catch on in Vilnius — and in the rest of the world.

And Sister Faustina, of course, returned to her gardens and greenhouse. It was May, a sweet season of blossoms and promises. Glad as she may have been to see the apple trees flowering, sister-gardener may have had a let-down feeling. The wonderful satisfaction of seeing Mercy Sunday celebrated publicly had come and gone.

In addition to all of that, the sister was suffering from great doubts once again. Sister Faustina was frightened by the remaining challenges of her Divine Mercy mission. They seemed too overwhelming for her poor powers. Rather than communicating directly with Jesus, she gradually began to simply recite prayers. One day, the Lord said, "You will prepare the world for My final coming." Sister Faustina heard and understood the implications of this awesome prophecy. But she was also frightened by it.

When she was trying to leave the chapel one time, she heard the words, "You intend to leave the chapel, but you shall not get away from Me, for I am everywhere. You cannot do anything of yourself, but with me you can do all things."

When she finally told her spiritual director of these new doubts about her mission, she realized that she was succumbing to temptations of fear. Father Sopocko told her to listen to Jesus once again. "Listen with your whole heart!" The next time Jesus appeared, Sister Faustina immediately collapsed at His feet and tearfully apologized. Jesus raised her up, allowed her to lay her head upon Him, and consoled her with comforting words. Jesus told her that she had nothing to fear. "You are my dwelling place and My constant repose," Christ said. "For your sake I will withold the hand which punishes; for your sake I bless the earth."

A new level of intimacy with Jesus began after that. After Holy Communion, she could often see within her heart Jesus as a beautiful one-year-old. One day, as she wrote in her diary, she had to fight an impulse to go and pick up the beautiful child from the altar during Mass. She had always loved children dearly. Sister Faustina was now twenty-nine. If she'd married, she undoubtedly would have had children.

But here was an exquisite and totally loveable child — Jesus. After a few moments, the Child came to the pew where Faustina was kneeling. He playfully put His hands upon her shoulder, leaned against her, and lifted His small face up to look at her intently. Just as quickly, however, the child was back upon the altar as the host was broken and eaten by the priest.

On May 12, 1935, Sister Faustina was awakened in the middle of the night. She saw that a man was dying in great torment with many souls emerging from a muddy abyss to testify against him. A woman, holding a pool of tears in her apron, testified against the man who had been, as Faustina saw, "full of the world's honors and applause." In Warsaw on this date, as Faustina later learned, the premier of the Republic of Poland, sixty-eight-year-old Jozef Pilsudski, died after an agonizing struggle.

More and more, Sister Faustina was aware of "souls" and the spiritual life of others. Her sisters at Vilnius noticed that she immediately understood their faults and the state of their souls. By nature, Faustina had always been talkative, animated, and ready to be involved with the social life of any group. But by the summer of 1935, Sister Faustina was noticeably more reserved, less "chatty." She was pleasant and spoke with others when the need arose. But she no longer initiated conversations. That was because even as she pulled carrots or cut lettuce to take in to the cook, she was united with Jesus in prayer for others.

Sunday, June 9, was the Feast of Pentecost. It was a warm day, and the convent gardener had waited until the sun was low to inspect her crops. As she walked along, noticing which rows would soon need water, she heard the Lord's voice. "By your entreaties, you and your companions shall obtain mercy for yourselves and for the world." She also instantly understood what was behind the phrase "you and your companions." She was to establish a new congregation, an order of sisters which would proclaim the Divine Mercy as its primary ministry. A new congregation!

Sister Faustina glanced at the sun as it was quietly setting behind a bank of trees. Her mind reeled with such a challenge. She no longer took notice of which cabbages looked especially dry and where some potatoes could be transplanted. With her right hand, she quickly dug for her rosary in the deep side pocket of her habit. "Oh, my Lord!" she prayed outloud. "I can't do it. I can't!"

Backtracking, Faustina made her way back through the garden, holding back tears of frustration and fear. "Do not fear," the Lord told her in a soothing, compassionate voice. "I Myself will make up for everything that is lacking in you."

Within a week or two, however, Sister Faustina shared this new dilemma with her spiritual director. To her shock, Father Sopocko already knew of this new request from the Lord. Her confessor advised her to be at peace with this new instruction from Jesus. If the Lord wanted her to found a new congregation, He would also eventually show her how it was to be done.

But Sister Faustina was still very young. By nature, she was emotionally intense and liked to act immediately when a decision was made. But she had no crystal ball. She couldn't see how she could establish a new religious order. When she tried to downplay the instructions of Jesus in her own mind, the Lord immediately appeared to her. "I desire that there be such a congregation," He said, correcting her.

The next day, a radiant, gloriously beautiful Jesus appeared to her during Mass. Jesus said that He wanted the congregation to be founded as soon as possible. At Communion time, a joy and a new confidence was kindled within her soul. Once again, she was ready for what needed to be done.

"What should I do?" she asked herself.

Sister Faustina didn't really know. The question was perpetually there — sitting at the edge of her consciousness, perched on top of her prayer intentions. "What should I do?" She asked herself the question over and over again.

It was a question which didn't seem to have an answer, a problem that lacked a visible solution. However, there had been other times when it seemed to her that answering God's call was impossible. She had found a way to enter the convent despite her family's objections and despite the lack of a dowry. She had found a way to live a contemplative prayer-life within an active order. The image of Jesus which she alone had seen had finally been painted by someone else. Sister Faustina was encouraged when she reminded herself of these things.

Although Sister Faustina was often freed of paralyzing anxiety about the new congregation, the question wasn't to be resolved in her own mind until shortly before her death.

August 5 was the congregation's special feast. Sister Faustina knelt in the small Vilnius chapel, praying intently. She told Our Lady of Mercy that she would find it difficult to separate from a community which enjoyed special protection from the Mother of God. The Blessed Virgin appeared. She came down to the kneeler where Sister Faustina knelt and embraced her. "I am Mother to you all, thanks to the unfathomable mercy of God," she said. "Most pleasing to me is that soul which faithfully carries out the will of God." Mary hadn't told Sister Faustina what to do. She had simply told her to do the will of God — when she understood what that will was. The Blessed Virgin also told the sister that she would be finally victorious in following Jesus if she would focus on the Passion of her Son.

On August 15, the sisters at Vilnius gathered to renew their vows. Mary, the Mother of God, suddenly appeared and came down to Sister Faustina's pew from the altar. She was dressed in white and blue, and her head was uncovered. Standing near her dear daughter, she placed her mantle over Faustina's head and said, "Offer these vows for Poland. Pray for her."

Events in neighboring Germany were deeply troubling to Poland and the rest of Europe. In August 1934 — one year earlier — Adolf Hitler had declared himself, *"Fuhrer und Reichskanzler"* (Leader and Reich Chancellor). In 1935, the Nazi Party rejected agreements Germany had made in the Versailles Treaty following the First World War. Compulsory military service was instituted in Germany, and an Air Force, the Luftwaffe, was also organized. Laws were passed in Germany which stripped Jews of many of their citizenship rights. War was on the horizon.

On August 25, Sister Faustina celebrated her thirtieth birthday, but even she may have overlooked the anniversary. It was hectic during this early harvest season. There were armloads of vegetables and fruits to pick and store every day. And the convent gardener directed her crew of girls to water the garden each day. Water gave life to plants sitting in the summer sun, just as God gives life and mercy to His children. But the wards didn't mind the hard, hot work. They loved Sister Faustina. She treated them with the deepest respect and with the protective affection of a big sister.

Faustina often started the girls singing while they all worked together in the garden. And sister-gardener seemed to know what the girls needed. She made sure that they had enough to eat and sometimes prepared Christmas packages for the girls who had no relatives to visit them. Several times, she urged particular girls to go to confession, or get a "bath," as she referred to the sacrament. She reminded them to make frequent little visits to the chapel and taught them prayers.

The wards saw that this lovely young woman had great joy in following Jesus. They wanted to be around her. Although the girls could see that Sister Faustina certainly wasn't very strong, she still saved the hardest, dirtiest jobs for herself. It was she who spread the manure when it was time to enrich the soil.

September 13, 1935, was a Friday. When Sister Faustina went to her cell in the evening, she was worn out. Her muscles ached and she wondered to herself how many years she would be able to direct the gardening before her weakening body gave out. She coughed a bit more now, and the coughing sapped her strength even further.

Suddenly, there was an angel, clothed in a dazzling robe. Sister Faustina understood immediately that his role was to carry out just punishments ascribed by heaven for wicked individuals. Bolts of lightning sprung into his hands from a cloud beneath his feet. When Faustina saw that the lightning of justice was about to strike in various places, she began to plead with the angel to wait. The world would do penance, she promised.

Then — just as suddenly — Sister Faustina was taken up to the throne of God. Overwhelmed by the greatness and holiness of Jesus and God the Father, she began to plead for God's mercy on the world with a prayer which seemed to be saying itself in her heart. At the same time, she saw that the angel was helpless to strike the guilty. "Never before had I prayed with such inner power as I did then," she wrote later in her diary.

The words that she heard and said in her heart were: "Eternal Father, I offer You the Body and Blood, Soul and Divinity of Your dearly beloved Son, Our Lord Jesus Christ, for our sins and those of the whole world; for the sake of His sorrowful Passion, have mercy on us and on the whole world."

The next morning, as she entered the chapel, Sister Faustina was given further directions about this new prayer. She was told, "Every time you enter the chapel, immediately recite the prayer which I taught you yesterday." She was told that the prayer would appease the wrath of God and that she should recite it for nine days as a novena on the beads of a rosary.

Before these prayers were said, an "Our Father," a "Hail Mary," and the "I Believe in God" were to be said on the three beads near the rosary's crucifix. She was then to say the first part of the prayer on the large beads separating the five decades and the shorter part of the prayer on each of the ten beads of each decade. At the end of all five "decades," she was to recite three times: "Holy God, Holy Mighty One, Holy Immortal One, have mercy on us and on the whole world."

In time, Jesus was to ask Sister Faustina to introduce this Divine Mercy Chaplet to her own community and to the world.

The chaplet quickly became a prayer that she said almost constantly. Within a year, thousands of copies of the prayer were printed and circulated on the reverse side of a Divine Mercy prayer-card. Father Sopocko had that done. And a few years after that, the chaplet was to circulate widely in a world miserably wounded by war. It was a prayer for mercy, an appeal to heaven which more and more believers desperately offered.

On the last day of September, 1935, everything that the Lord had been telling her and asking of her in the previous several years seemed to fit together. They were like the small, colorful pieces of glass which, when assembled by an artist, create a glorious picture in stained glass

First — in 1931, at Plock, she had been shown the image of the Divine Mercy and told to "paint an image according to the pattern you see with the signature: Jesus, I trust in You." She did not, as it happened, personally paint the image. However, she directed the painting in progress and then worked for its public display and veneration.

Then later, Jesus asked Sister Faustina to become a "victim soul." She agreed to suffer great agonies of all sorts in order to unite her sufferings with those of Jesus. The goal was to help save souls. Jesus then gave her Mercy prayers to pray in conjunction with her new ministry of suffering for souls. After that, Jesus directed her to have the Second Sunday of Easter established and celebrated as a "Feast of Mercy." And later still, she received the Chaplet of Mercy and the Novena to the Divine Mercy. These she began to pray herself. Then, when she was directed by Jesus to do so, she shared them anonymously with her community and with the larger world.

There had been so many profound and challenging messages given to the slender young sister whose job descriptions had directed her to the convent kitchens, laundry rooms, and the gardens. She was a sister who worked with her hands. But for many years Jesus had been quietly working with her, forming her into His "Apostle of Mercy."

"O my God, I am conscious of my mission in the Holy Church," she wrote in her tight, neat script one night. "It is my constant endeavor to plead for mercy for the world. I unite myself closely with Jesus and stand before Him as an atoning sacrifice on behalf of the world. God will refuse me nothing when I entreat Him with the voice of His Son."

Finally, she knew the whole of it. She understood why God had called her even as a very young child in Glogowiec. In October and November, she focused more and more on the last part of her Mercy mission — that of laying the groundwork for a congregation of sisters who would devote themselves to interceding for mercy for an increasingly wicked world. In November, she began the second notebook of her diary. She spent about a month writing out a rule for this future order.

"There will never be any splendid houses, but only a small church with a small community consisting of a few souls, not more than ten, plus two externs to look after external affairs," wrote Sister Faustina in her diary. "Each house will be independent of the others, although they will be closely united by the rule, the vows and the spirit." Thinking more and more deeply about this future community, she stipulated that the community was to be truly cloistered, with a dark cloth covering the grill and all conversations strictly limited. There were to be no distinctions between the sisters — "no mothers, no reverends, no venerables, but all will be equal even though there might be great differences in their parentage."

Sister Faustina poured her heart and inspirations into the rule within her diary. The congregation — the flesh and blood actualization of her plans — was not to exist for many years. But the spirit of it had already been born. And Sister Faustina seemed to believe that she could reach out and touch the face of the future.

On December 21, just before Christmas, Father Sopocko asked Sister Faustina to visit a certain dilapitated house in Vilnius which she had seen in a vision. It was to be, she had been told, the convent for the new congregation.

Agreeing, Sister Faustina threw a heavy cloak around her. Cold, sharp winds swept across the Neris River, which snaked its way through the old medieval city. They seemed to pierce Sister Faustina's chest like icy daggers. She coughed often, but followed Father Sopocko down a narrow street. Finally, he stopped and pointed at some snow-covered ruins. He had recognized the place from the description she had given to him.

"Yes! That's it!" she said, nodding to make sure he understood the words she sputtered between fits of coughing.

She'd been disappointed when she'd learned that this broken-down place would be the convent of the new order. But Jesus promised to bless it and the surrounding neighborhood. And Father Sopocko later discussed with her the arrangment of cells within this future house of religious women. But she was less and less concerned about when this new work would see the light of day.

"Do not fear anything," Jesus had told her. "I am with you. These matters are in My hands and I will bring them to fruition according to My mercy, for nothing can oppose My will."

Sister Faustina thought of that consoling promise many times during the next ten days. As it always did, the Christmas season brought such joy. And when she thought of those hands of Jesus which would bring the Mercy Mission to fruition, she smiled. Who could forget that those hands had also been the tiny hands of a beautiful baby born to embrace the world.

12

Visions of Infinite Mercy

"I desire that the whole world know My infinite mercy. I desire to grant unimaginable graces to those souls who trust in My mercy" — Words of Jesus to Faustina, **Diary, 687**.

The New Year — 1936 — wasn't very old when Sister Mary Faustina again began to agonize over the congregation which Jesus wanted her to found. The peace she'd felt in December melted in January like a dusting of snow under the mid-morning sun.

What should she do? She was absolutely certain that the Lord was telling her to leave her own order to establish a new one. Jesus wanted a contemplative congregation. It was to intercede for and witness to God's divine mercy. But even as she felt committed to following the command of Christ, she also felt bound to the Sisters of Our Lady of Mercy. She had made final vows in this order! And she had spent eleven years of her life within the congregation. It was her home, her family. The dilemma was very, very hard on Sister Faustina.

On the morning of January 8, she pulled on snow boots, her warmest coat, gloves, and an extra scarf to cover her mouth and set out for Vilnius. She needed to talk with fifty-nine-year-old Archbishop Romuald Jalbrzykowski again. He was the archbishop of Vilnius. During the summer before, Faustina had gone to confession to the archbishop. She had discussed the Divine Mercy image, devotions, and the question of a new congregation. Like Father Sopocko, the archbishop had thought that the congregation idea was probably a temptation, since she was solemnly vowed to the Sisters of Our Lady of Mercy.

After she arrived, Sister Faustina took a deep breath and told the archbishop that Jesus was still urging her to found the new order. This time, his response was more gentle. And yet, after he'd heard her out, the archbishop still felt that it would be wrong and unwise to move too quickly.

"As for prayer," he said, "I give my permission and even encourage you, Sister, to pray as much as possible for the world and to beg God's mercy, as mercy is what we all need. But as regards this congregation, wait a while, Sister, so that all things may arrange themselves favorably. This thing is good in itself, but there is no need to hurry. If it is God's will, it will be done, whether it be a little sooner or a little later."

So, Sister Faustina was calmed down by the time she headed back to the convent — especially after Jesus immediately reassured her that "I speak through My representatives" in the matter of the new congregation. And so, during the first month of the year, Sister Faustina enjoyed some mid-winter's peace with regard to her mission.

On January 29, however, a different burden replaced the one taken from her. She had a vision of Father Sopocko, her spiritual director and confessor, suffering great mental anguish and ordeals. The sister could see that this man's plight was terrible. He was her good friend, and she pitied him in his present state.

"Why do you treat him like that?" she complained to Jesus. When Jesus explained that Father Sopocko was suffering to win heavenly crowns, she understood. This priest, she knew, was a very pure soul. His sufferings had a great purpose. "I rejoice greatly that God has allowed me to know such souls," she wrote later in her diary.

Nonetheless, on February 2, she begged the Lord to remove a particular hardship from the priest and Jesus agreed to it. With the gift of inner knowledge which was operating in her more and more, she could see how hard things were for her confessor.

Inevitably, however, the issue of the new congregation emerged again. During the first few days of March, her frustrations reached the boiling point. She could see no solution to the difficulty. "You urge me on the one hand and hold me back and restrain me on the other," she fumed to her Lord. And that was true. Heaven had sent her the inspiration for the new congregation. But Jesus had also told her to listen to "My representatives" — the priests.

There was no attempt to block Faustina's impulse to follow the mandate Jesus had given her. But founding a new congregation was a much more complicated issue than having a painting painted or prayer cards printed. The priests counseling her hesitated, waited, and urged her to be patient.

As time went on, Sister Faustina raised the issue again and again with her superior and Father Sopocko. "I felt that Sister Faustina, as a simple nun without any material support, could not do this," Father Sopocko explained many years later. "I counseled her not to leave her congregation."

And the archbishop urged her to move cautiously, to wait for the right moment.

Mother Superior Borgia quickly noticed that her young gardener was too pale, too down-in-the-mouth — even for winter-time. She knew about Sister Faustina's sense that Jesus was calling her to a new religious order. Father Sopocko had told Sister Faustina to tell her superior about the Lord's instructions.

"Is there anything I can do, Sister? You don't look well," Mother told Faustina. She knew that this sister's health was terribly fragile. She ordered the kitchen to prepare a cup of hot milk each night for Sister Faustina. Sister Faustina smiled, grateful for the gesture and the milk. But she doubted if all the warm milk in Vilnius could give her a good night of sleep. Only one "medicine" could help. The congregation question needed to be resolved.

One day, she had a vision about the future congregation and described what she had seen in her diary.

"I saw a small chapel in which six sisters were receiving Holy Communion from our confessor [Father Sopocko] who was wearing a surplice and stole. There were no decorations and no kneelers in the chapel. After Holy Communion, I saw the Lord Jesus as He is represented in the image. Jesus was walking away, and I called to Him, 'How can You pass me by and not say anything to me, Lord? Without You, I shall do nothing; You must stay with me and bless me, and this community and my country as well.' Jesus made the sign of the cross and said, 'Do not fear anything; I am always with you.' "

Three weeks later, Sister Faustina was thinking about the challenges facing her. It was March 18 and the middle of Lent. Her confessor had told her not to cut down on food because of the delicacy of her health. But in many other ways, she was burdened with sufferings.

She could not stand the anxiety any longer. So the troubled young woman prayed and asked Jesus to make things happen. It even occurred to her that being expelled from her present order was one more way to settle the thing. She was certain that Christ could arrange that — if it was needed.

On the following day, Mother Superior told Sister Faustina that she would be transferred to Warsaw. Mother General Michael Moraczewska had made the decision. Faustina presumed that this was the "sign" that she had begged Jesus to give her. "I won't need to go to Warsaw," she told her superior, "since I will be leaving the congregation."

Sister Faustina believed that Jesus wanted her to found a new order of nuns in Vilnius. Mother Borgia knew that. And she knew that someone as conscientious as Faustina had to obey the Lord's leadings. But she didn't want to lose her. Sister Faustina was a model nun. And she was a precious gift to her congregation.

"Why don't you go to Warsaw anyway, Sister," the older nun urged. "If you eventually leave us, it wouldn't delay you very much."

Sister Faustina was very quiet for a moment. She looked down at her hands and then stared at the simple silver ring that the bishop had slipped onto her finger on the day of her solemn vows. She sighed heavily, thinking of the many times in recent months that her Spouse had spoken with her about the new congregation. She was distressed that she had not yet been able to act on His requests.

"Very well, Mother," she responded finally. "I will go with Mother General to Warsaw. I'm sure that Jesus will show me how the matter will be arranged. But right now . . . I don't know." Obedience — it was the habit of many years. Sister Faustina said "Yes." She wanted to obey her superior as long as she was a member of the congregation. After taking her leave of Mother Borgia, Sister Faustina went to her cell to begin packing her few things. She had been at Vilnius for almost three years.

In a religious congregation, transfers of sisters from one convent and location to another were more or less routine. And in her almost ten years in the convent, Sister Faustina herself had been transferred many times. But for many reasons, this move ordered for the convent gardener was quite painful. There was a melancholy feeling about it for almost everyone.

Sister Faustina felt the pain first of all. She would no longer have the support and religious counseling of Father Sopocko. For so many years, she had prayed and longed for a holy and balanced spiritual director. She had seen him in visions, and finally, the Lord had led her to him. Now she was leaving that director.

When the girls who were wards heard about the change of assignment of the nun they loved so much, they were also very upset.

"Meeting Mother General, we asked her when Sister Faustina would be coming back," wrote Hedwig Owar, one of the wards. "She told us: 'My dear children, I don't come to take the sisters out for a walk.' We understood that Sister Faustina would not be coming back to us and we cried."

On the evening before she left for Warsaw, an elderly nun tearfully intercepted Sister Faustina and grabbed her hand. Apparently, it was sixty-eight-year-old Sister Antonina Grejwul, a native of Vilnius. Faustina reported the encounter in her diary.

"She said that she had already been suffering interiorly for several years, that it seemed to her that all her confessions had been bad, and that she had doubts as to whether the Lord Jesus had forgiven her." It wasn't the first time that Sister Faustina had been sought out for spiritual advice by one of her sisters.

Father Sopocko later recalled that "her co-sisters even of the first choir often turned to her for advice in spiritual matters and always received a sensible answer. I also know that sisters turned to her in various painful matters, when sad and in need of advice and comfort, and that they always received such comfort."

Once again, Sister Faustina was a source of comfort. She simply told the older nun to explain her difficulty to her confessor.

But Antonina wouldn't let Faustina go. She had aired her doubts in the confessional, she said, but the priests were not able to dispel her anxieties. "I know that the Lord Jesus speaks to you, Sister," Sister Antonina sobbed. She begged Sister Faustina to ask Jesus if her sins were indeed wiped away. That night, Sister Faustina did speak with Jesus about the old nun's problem and later shared what Jesus had said. "Tell her that her disbelief wounds My heart more than the sins she committed." That was the message Faustina had for the happy Antonina the next day.

Because the Mother General apparently had further business in Vilnius, on March 21, Sister Faustina boarded the train to Warsaw without a sister-companion. But, as she recorded in her diary later, she was not alone. One of the seven spirits or angels closest to God accompanied her. "I constantly saw him beside me when I was riding on the train. I saw an angel standing on every church we passed, but surrounded by a light which was paler than that of the spirit who was accompanying me on the journey, and each of these spirits who were guarding the churches bowed his head to the spirit who was near me."

Warsaw was simply a stopover for Sister Faustina. Within a few days, she was told that her next assignment was at Walendow, a tiny rural community, about twelve miles from Warsaw. Sister Faustina accepted the assignment despite the fact that she'd told Mother Borgia that she would soon be leaving.

Sister was welcomed in a generous and friendly way at Walendow. The sisters there had heard a few things about her spiritual gifts and dedication. But the farming and gardening work which all of the Walendow sisters were shouldering was just too much for the fragile Sister Faustina. The nuns were forced to work all day — every day! At this house, they needed all the funds they could get from gardening.

When the superior asked her to dust the walls, she asked if she could have another job instead. But the superior insisted and Faustina did her best, offering her exhaustion and nausea as Lenten sacrifices. Inevitably, Sister Faustina got so sick and weak that she soon had to go to bed. Right before Easter, she went to confession to Father Aloysius Bukowski, S.J., and shared her commitment to begin a new congregation. Angrily, he shouted at her, reminding her of her perpetual vows. Then, he accused her of heresy and of perpetuating an illusion. "Give no thought to these things and put them completely out of your mind," he insisted. Shaken and embarrassed, she left the confessional and pondered the issue.

The Lord had told her that he would speak through His "representatives." Father Bukowski was surely one of those "representatives." Sister Faustina tried to do what she was told. She tried to get the idea of a new order out of her mind. She felt ensnared by conflicting commitments and she begged God to free her. She was freed when she received the Eucharist — freed from everything but a growing longing to be with Jesus forever.

Soon after that, however, Jesus appeared again to His "Secretary of Mercy." "Tell the confessor that this work is Mine and that I am using you as a lowly instrument," He told her. When Father Bukowski came from Derdy a few days later, she overcame the sting of his earlier remarks. Right away, she went to him for confession. His attitude, this time, was "quite different," she noted in her diary. Father Bukowski explained that he'd tried to warn her because illusions can fool even holy people. "God will find a way to bring about His work," he advised her.

Though she was again soon reassigned to Derdy, a charming, little country house set near a forest, she was only there for several weeks. The superiors now realized that Sister Faustina's illness was very serious and that she would require constant medical supervision. This meant a move back to Cracow.

On the morning of May 11, Faustina stood on the steps of the convent at Derdy. She was saying good-bye to a close friend from novitiate days, twenty-seven-year-old Sister Justine Golofit. They laughed and talked for a few moments about their novitiate days together in the kitchen in Cracow.

Then Sister Faustina's voice became more serious. "Justine, I have to tell you," she said gently. "I will die in the autumn two years from now. I won't see you again in this life, my dear friend!" When Justine began to cry, Faustina tried to console her, reminding her that they would indeed be together again with Jesus. But when it was time to leave, she cautioned her friend: "Don't tell anyone while I'm still alive." Faustina then smiled that quick, engaging smile that was so familiar to her friend. She hugged Justine quickly and headed for the car.

Though Faustina had been thoroughly enchanted with Derdy, the move back to Cracow was encouraging. It seemed to her that in Cracow she would finally be able to see progress made on the new congregation. She told

Father Andrasz, the convent confessor, that she had decided to leave. However, when she felt God's presence abandon her spirit on the following day, she decided to postpone the matter again. But that didn't mean that she was liberated from the burden imposed on her by Christ.

She didn't know where to turn for an answer. How could she honor her solemn vows to her congregation *and* obey the instructions of the Lord at the same time? It didn't seem possible. As much as they could, Sister Faustina's superiors sympathized with her dilemma. And they tried hard to ease the psychic toll it was taking on her. They knew that Faustina felt as though she was being torn in half.

"Mother, what do you think?" Sister Faustina asked Mother Michael Moraczewska one day. She had told her about the many messages and visions she'd received in regard to the congregation. Mother Michael looked at her, shaking her head in astonishment. Many years ago, she had admitted this remarkably holy young woman to the convent as a skinny, penniless girl.

"Sister," Mother Michael said, "I am locking you in the tabernacle with the Lord Jesus; wherever you go from there, that will be the will of God." But during the summer of 1936, there was no resolution! Action on the new congregation seemed to be permanently on hold. No answer came to the question she continued to ask herself, "What should I do?"

Sister Faustina, who was serving again as gardener, continued to endure the jibes and sardonic sneers of her sisters at Cracow. Some of them thought that she was putting on a show, separating herself from them, making herself "holier" than anyone else.

In early August, Sister was given an envelope postmarked from Vilnius. The handwriting was familiar. She knew right away who it was from. But the package itself was larger than an ordinary letter could make it. She ripped it open when she had a private moment. It was beautiful brochure entitled "*Milosierdzie Boze*" ("The Divine Mercy") with a subtitle explaining that the contents would provide a theological and practical study of the Divine Mercy. The brochure was written by Father Sopocko and carried Archbishop Jalbrzykowski's imprimatur. There was a print of the Divine Mercy image on the front. Father Sopocko explained in his note that the brochures had been printed in Vilnius. They were being received very enthusiastically, he told her.

It was the kind of lift that Sister Faustina needed. A huge smile broke out upon her face and she sat to reread the note again. She tucked the letter and brochure down into her side pocket near her rosary, and then headed to the kitchen where she had some duties. "I know you are spreading this good news about Your mercy, Jesus," she whispered to Him as though they were conspirators. "I just wish that I could help You to move it along a little faster."

On the first Friday of September, Sister Faustina had a vivid and terrifying vision of Our Lady. Her bared breast was pierced by a sword and she was weeping bitterly, even as she attempted to prevent a great punishment from befalling Poland. Sister Faustina began to pray with great emotion for her native land. And a few days later, Jesus had another message for her about prayer. The sister was on her way down a corridor to the kitchen when she heard Jesus speak:

"Unceasingly say the chaplet that I have taught you," He said. "Whoever will recite it will receive great mercy at the hour of death. Priests will recommend it to sinners as their last hope of salvation. Even if there were a sinner most hardened, if he recites this chaplet only once, he will receive grace from My infinite mercy. I desire that the whole world know My infinite mercy. I desire to grant unimaginable graces to those souls who trust in My mercy."

On September 14, Archbishop Romuald Jalbrzykowski of Vilnius interrupted his travels to stop by for a visit. Sister Faustina spoke with him briefly, sharing her continuing pain over the congregation Jesus wanted. He told her what he'd said before, but he said it even more gently. "Sister, be at peace; if this is within the plans of divine providence, it will come about. In the meantime, Sister, pray for a clearer outward sign."

The archbishop didn't miss the fact that Sister Faustina's youthful, freckled face was drawn and very pale. Those beautiful gray-green eyes seemed tired. She'd clearly lost weight and appeared to be restless. And yet, it was a restlessness to accomplish the will of Jesus as she was interpreting it. He knew that. There wasn't a self-centered bone in Sister Faustina's body. The archbishop had sensed that the first time he spoke with her.

"How's Sister Faustina feeling? She seems ill," Archbishop Jalbrzykowski said later when he talked with Mother Raphael Buczynska. When the superior said that the doctors couldn't pinpoint any cause for Sister's failing health, the archbishop suggested that they consult with a specialist. No one could fail to see that she coughed frequently, and that she was losing weight and strength.

On September 19, Sister Faustina was sent to a lung specialist. Dr. Adam Silberg soon diagnosed her illness as tuberculosis. He told her superiors that she should be isolated from the other sisters so that the contagious disease would not spread further. Six days later, Sister Faustina suffered paralyzing pains for almost three hours. The pains were so severe that she was not able to move at all. The attack was the bitter foretaste of many more attacks to come. And not yet knowing that, the shaky hand of Sister

Faustina soon wrote in her diary "if after such suffering death does not come, then how great the sufferings of death must be!"

It seemed that great sufferings and great joy seemed to alternate for her. Soon after the painful attack, Jesus gave her a summarizing message about His Feast of Mercy. She was so happy to hear it and recorded it word for word in the diary.

"I desire that the Feast of Mercy be a refuge and shelter for all souls, and especially for poor sinners," He said. "On that day, the very depths of My tender mercy are open. I pour out a whole ocean of graces upon those souls who approach the fount of My mercy. The souls that will go to Confession and receive Holy Communion shall obtain complete forgiveness of sins and punishment. On that day are open all the divine floodgates through which graces flow."

But such reassurances about the Divine Mercy mission seemed to be her only source of joy and support. Even though the sanitorium had made it clear that Sister Faustina was seriously ill, the response of some of her sisters was strangely cold — and detached!

When Sister Faustina admitted to Mother Raphael that she felt constant pain and fatigue, Mother told her that she should get used to suffering. On another occasion, the ailing and exhausted sister went to the kitchen to ask for a little food. She didn't have the energy to stay up for dinner. The doctors had instructed Sister Faustina's superiors to provide her with complete rest and isolation. But their orders were somehow downgraded to a regime of rest and moderate activity. Sister Faustina was told by an irritated cook: "But you are not ill, Sister! They only wanted you to have some rest. So, they made up this illness."

Such insensitivities stung her, but she gradually understood that her only true comforts would come from heaven. On September 29, the Feast of the Archangels, St. Michael appeared. "The Lord has ordered me to take special care of you," he said, shining with a radiance and strength that almost took her breath away. "Know that you are hated by evil; but do not fear — 'Who is like God!'"

On October 5, another letter came from Vilnius from Father Sopocko. Again, Faustina tore it open, anxious to read what her spiritual director had to say. Father Sopocko was so busy with the Divine Mercy message. He told her that he was intending to publish a holy card of the Merciful Jesus. He wanted to have a copy of a prayer which she had written in her diary. If the archbishop approved, he wanted to have the prayer printed on the reverse side of the card.

Sister Faustina was so elated with this new bit of news. It gave her such joy to know that Father Sopocko was making progress in sharing the Divine Mercy message. Later in October, however, Jesus asked Faustina to share the chaplet within the convent. "Go to the Superior and tell her that I want all the sisters and wards to say the chaplet which I have taught you," Jesus told her.

Sister Faustina bit her lip with anxiety. Many of her sisters, she realized, didn't really trust her. They presumed that her illnesses were feigned in order to provide her with more free time. The life of a second-choir nun was extremely busy and tiring. Even Mother Rose didn't know what to make of Faustina, and Sister Faustina was aware of it. Asking these sisters to recite a prayer personally given to her by Jesus would only add to their distrust.

For a while, this sister stalled. Typically, she was so obedient to Jesus, but she told herself that such a project should be discussed with her spiritual director. Soon, however, the "Secretary of Divine Mercy" knew that Jesus was very displeased. The sense of His presence disappeared. She didn't receive Holy Communion for four days, thinking that she was unworthy. When she finally did go to confession and told Father Andrasz about her disobedience, he urged her to be true to the requests of Jesus. Soon she went to talk with Mother about the chaplet. Nothing immediately came of her attempt, and there was little Sister Faustina could do—except pray.

For that reason, Sister Faustina looked forward to her annual eight-day retreat, which began on October 20. Another Jesuit, Father Walter Wojton, directed the retreat for the sisters at Cracow. During the retreat, she often experienced deep union with God. She learned more during these occasions than she could have learned in long hours of intellectual inquiry, she reported in her diary. But she also had a terrifying experience of hell. Because it was so frightening, Jesus had to command her to write about it in her diary.

Hell, she wrote, "is a place of great torture; how awesomely large and extensive it is!" The six major kinds of torture, she said, include the loss of God, perpetual remorse of conscience, the permanence of hell itself, a fire that penetrates but doesn't destroy, continual darkness, and a suffocating smell. Sister Faustina said that she surely would have died at the sight of these tortures and others, if God had not sustained her. She wrote — at God's command, she explained — so that "no soul may find an excuse by saying there is no hell, or that nobody has ever been there and so no one can say what it is like."

During the same retreat, however, the terrifying look at hell was offset by the hope and encouragement of another vision. Jesus explained even further how His divine mercy was to be exercised. There were three ways of doing this, He told Sister Faustina — through deed, word, and prayer. Jesus explained that He did indeed want the celebration of His Feast of Mercy and the veneration of the Divine Mercy image. But, He also wanted to see mercy shown on earth "because even the strongest faith is of no avail without works."

Late in November, Sister Faustina wrote in her diary that she'd been receiving the stigmata pains on Fridays since the end of September. The stigmata wounds were hidden — no one saw them or was aware that she shared these wound of Christ. "There is no outward indication of these sufferings," she wrote. "What will come later, I do not know. All this, for the sake of souls."

On November 27, Sister Faustina was confined to bed by her illness. Suddenly, as she wrote, "I was in heaven in spirit, and I saw the inconceivable beauties and the happiness that awaits us after death." She saw the souls of heaven giving constant praise to God. "I rejoice," she said, "immensely in His greatness and am delighted that I am so little because, since I am little, He carries me in His arms and holds me close to His heart." She sat up in bed later that night, bent over her diary. In the dim light thrown from her table lamp, she wrote about this vision of heaven and the renewed passion it gave her for the message of mercy.

On Wednesday, December 9, Sister Faustina was taken to the sanatorium in nearby Pradnik. Mother Superior told her that Mother General wanted her to undergo a three-month regime of treatment for her tuberculosis. Faustina had been given no warning that this hospitalization was coming and the news made her nervous. She'd never been in a hospital before. But Jesus calmed her fears, and later in the afternoon, Sister Chrysostom drove her to the clinic, where she was admitted to a private room.

Sister took quick note of her surroundings. Her room was near the men's ward. She noted in her diary with some disgust, that "I didn't know that men were such chatterboxes." What was most tragic, however, was what was *not* said.

"My Jesus, how little these people talk about You," she observed. "They talk about everything but You, Jesus. And if they talk so little [about You], it is quite probable that they do not think about You at all. The whole world interests them; but about their Creator, there is silence."

Hours after she went to bed on Friday night, December 11, Sister Faustina was awakened from a sound sleep. She knew in her heart that she was to pray for a dying person. She got up, knelt by her bed, and began to pray with great concentration. On the following day, as she walked through the women's ward, she saw the woman she'd prayed for.

Sister Faustina walked over to the woman's bed and asked the Lord once again to shower His mercy upon this human being. The woman's eyes fluttered open and she stared at Faustina. Sister smiled, took her hand, and began to pray the chaplet once again. Before she'd finished, the woman's eyes closed, and Sister Faustina saw the woman's body relax in death.

Touched by the experience, Sister spoke to no one but returned to her room. She had accompanied the dying and prayed for them for many years — even as a teenager. "At the hour of their death," Jesus said to her later, "I defend as My own glory every soul that will say this chaplet; or when others say it for a dying person, the indulgence is the same."

Slowly, the tubercular patient became used to the hospital routine. She was treated kindly and with professionalism. But being away from her convent and being in a private room were isolating experiences. On Friday, December 18, she was a bit depressed. Besides the medical staff, no one had visited her for a week. It was one week before Christmas, and memories of home and family may have been surfacing.

When Faustina complained of her loneliness to Jesus, He said, "Isn't it enough for you that I visit you every day?" Chastened, she apologized and her homesickness disappeared. Even so, Faustina cried with happiness when Sister Chrysostom came on December 23, bringing her some apples, lemons, and a tiny Christmas tree. Faustina learned that she'd been given permission to spend Christmas back at the convent.

On Christmas Eve, Sister Cajetan came for her. As they drove home, Faustina gazed out at the snow-covered streets, thinking about Mary, who was also traveling on the day before Jesus' birth. Back in the convent at Cracow, Sister Faustina went quickly to the chapel. In her years of convent life, she had made it a custom on Christmas Eve to share the wafer in a spiritual, imaginary way with her loved ones before supper.

She thought of the table at home at Glogowiec. Around the table, she imagined her father and her mother, who was well again. Also there were her older sisters, Josephine and Genevieve. Around the table she moved, sharing the Christmas wafer in her heart with Natalia, Mary, dear Wanda, and with her brothers, Stanley and Mecislaus.

At Midnight Mass on Christmas Eve, Sister Faustina enjoyed a vision of another family — the Holy Family.

"A moment before Elevation I saw the Mother of God and the Infant Jesus and the good Old Man [St. Joseph]. The Most Holy Mother spoke these words to me: 'My daughter, Faustina, take this most precious Treasure,' and she gave me the Infant Jesus. When I took Jesus in my arms, my soul felt such unspeakable joy that I am unable to describe it."

On December 27, Sister Damiana Ziolek took Sister Faustina back to the sanatorium. In the taxi with them, however, was a woman and a new-born infant. The sisters had offered to share the ride with the happy woman, who was taking the baby to a local church to be baptized.

The baby had been abandoned at the convent gate a day or two earlier. The woman, who lived near the convent, heard about it. She had no children and readily agreed to receive this Christmas "gift" as her own child. On the way to the church, sisters Faustina and Damiana smiled at the new mother, who cooed and cuddled her precious one.

On New Year's Eve, Sister Faustina kept another of her own traditions. She spent the whole evening praying for special intentions. At midnight, she was overcome with some fear. She had some idea about the things which would happen to her soon.

Despite the best efforts of the Pradnik medical staff, her health was failing. She knew that was true. She knew how much suffering was in store for her in 1937, and for a few moments, it terrified her.

13

Joy and Sorrow Go Hand in Hand

"It pleased Me to carry out this work of mercy precisely through you who are nothing but misery itself. Do not fear; I will not leave you alone. Do whatever you can in this matter; I will accomplish everything that is lacking in you. You know what is within your power to do; do that" — Words of Jesus to Faustina, **Diary, 881**.

"Resolutions for the year 1937, day 1, month 1."

Sister Faustina penned these words at the top of a page in her diary on New Year's Day, 1937. Cold winds and flurries swirled outside the Pradnik clinic. She was a patient in Tuberculosis Ward I, and was very much aware that her illness was fatal. In fact, she also knew that she'd have only one more chance after this one to write "New Year's resolutions."

Her program was tough, thorough, well-thought-out. And it was totally based upon what she believed was the will of Jesus for her.

   I.   Strict observance of silence — interior silence.

  II.   To see the image of God in every sister; all love of neighbor must flow from this motive.

 III.   To do the will of God faithfully at every moment of my life and to live by this.

 IV.   To give a faithful account of everything to the spiritual director and not to undertake anything of importance without a clear understanding with him. I shall try to clearly lay bare to him the most secret depth of my soul, bearing in mind that I am dealing with God Himself, and that His representative is just a human being, and so I must pray daily that he be given light.

  V.   During the evening examination of conscience, I am to ask myself the question: What if He were to call me today?

VI. Not to look for God far away, but within my own being to abide with Him alone.

VII. In sufferings and torments, to take refuge in the tabernacle and to be silent.

Sister Faustina continued in the same vein with another six resolutions. No one could say that she was easing up on herself just because she was extremely ill. She wanted to be "perfect"; she wanted to be as much like Jesus as she could be. But the fragile sister who demanded so much of herself was still generous with her time and her prayers.

"Today, a girl came to see me," she noted in her diary on the third or fourth day of January. "I saw that she was suffering, but not so much in body as in soul. I comforted her as much as I could, but my words of consolation were not enough. She was a poor orphan with a soul plunged in bitterness and pain. She opened her soul to me and told me everything. I understood that, in this case, simple words of consolation would not be enough. I fervently interceded with the Lord for that soul and offered Him my joy so that He would give it to her and take all feeling of joy away from me. And the Lord heard my prayer: I was left only with the consolation that she had been consoled."

Sister Faustina longed for a resolution to her anxieties about the congregation. On the first Sunday of the month, she burst into tears during the time of adoration. She begged the Lord to inspire her superiors and her confessors to support the congregation. After all, she tearfully complained, they were the ones who were delaying the work! The Lord calmed her, urging her to "be at peace; it will not be long now."

The cold days of early January passed by slowly, as they do for those who must spend most of their days indoors. In her clinic room, Sister Faustina listened to hymns on the radio and to news reports. Germany, she understood, was demanding that Poland give the city of Gdansk back, since it had once been under German control. But Poland refused to do it, and the Nazi-controlled government was raising its fists in temper.

For the young tubercular patient, the day's high point was attending Mass and receiving Holy Communion. But since the chapel was about seventy steps from her room, in another building, getting to Mass wasn't always possible.

Her physician, Dr. Adam Silberg, a recent convert to Catholicism, discussed the dilemma about getting to Mass with Sister Faustina. At forty, Dr. Silberg was the director of the sanatorium and lived on the grounds with his wife and son, Kazimierz. He was aware that Faustina's condition was very serious and incurable. He had met and befriended many dying patients during his years of medical practice, but this young woman's spirituality fascinated him. They had many conversations on spiritual questions, and Sister Faustina didn't hesitate to make her needs clear to him.

"I begged him not to make it difficult for me to go to Holy Communion, for it would have an adverse effect on the treatment," she reported in her diary. The doctor understood that it was a great heartbreak to her when she could not receive the Eucharist. "All right, Sister," he agreed, "when the weather is fine, and it isn't raining, and you feel all right, then, Sister, please go; but you must weigh these matters in your conscience."

Faustina made it a matter of obedience to live by Dr. Silberg's guidelines. Immediately, however, she told Jesus that if He wanted her to receive Communion, He was to make sure that she had no fever and felt well in the mornings. And Jesus often arranged it that way.

On January 14, Jesus appeared in a bright robe and girded with a golden belt. He asked her why she was giving in to thoughts of fear about her new congregation.

She answered that "this work frightens me. You know that I am incapable of carrying it out. You see very well that I am not in good health, that I have no education, that I have no money, that I am an abyss of misery, that I fear contacts with people." All of her concerns flowed out to Him. Why was God giving her such contradictory messages? She honestly didn't know. But then, she said quietly, "Jesus, I desire only You. You can release me from this."

The Lord didn't deny Sister's words. He agreed that she was very weak and helpless. But, He explained, "it pleased Me to carry out this work of mercy precisely through you who are nothing but misery itself. Do not fear; I will not leave you alone. Do whatever you can in this matter; I will accomplish everything that is lacking in you. You know what is within your power to do; do that."

Then, as she noted in her diary, His look of kindness filled her once again with joy, strength, and power to act. However, she was nonetheless surprised and even a bit sad that He was not going to release her from her mission. "I see that joy and sorrow go hand in hand," she observed.

On January 21, she was blessed all day with a wondrous unity with the Lord. But in the evening, the hospital chaplain came to visit and talk with her. "After we had talked for a while," she noted later in her diary, "I felt my spirit beginning to immerse itself in God, and I began to lose all sense of what was happening around me."

Such experiences of ecstasy had happened before. And Sister Faustina understood what was taking place. But she was with someone else on this occasion and she was embarrassed!

"I ardently implored Jesus, 'Give me the ability to talk.' And the Lord granted that I could talk freely with him. But there was a moment when I could not understand what the priest was saying." She blushed and apologized to the priest. The ecstatic union with God, she already knew, was a wonderful grace for the living person but was "imperfect." The senses acted imperfectly, she said, and when the soul is truly absorbed in God, the senses don't function.

"When such a grace visits me, I want to be alone, and I ask Jesus to protect me from the eyes of creatures," she noted later.

By January 27, Sister Faustina could state in her diary that "I feel considerable improvement in my health. Jesus is bringing me from the gates of death to life, because there was so little left but for me to die, and lo, the Lord grants me the fullness of life." But the recovering patient was ambivalent about this recovery. "I have desired death so much!" she noted later. It was a desire that she felt more and more.

"As I sat down to a very tasty breakfast," she wrote during the same period, "I said to the Lord, 'Thank you for these gifts, but my heart is dying of longing for You, and nothing earthly is tasty to me. I desire the food of Your love.'"

Soon after that, Sister Faustina heard Jesus say that He wanted her to be His spiritual spouse. This meant that the Lord wanted Faustina to be united with Him more deeply than ever. United in suffering, united in the love of God, and united in showing His mercy to the world. Fear overwhelmed her when she thought about this awesome request — and yet, she was also confused. At her perpetual vows, she had already become the spouse of the Lord. Gradually, however, she realized that Jesus intended something else in this special relationship.

On February 7, Sister Faustina opened a note from the Mother Superior. She learned that she was no longer to visit the dying in the clinic. From then on, however, Sister Faustina frequently sensed when someone was dying. Immediately, she began to intercede for them and sometimes found herself transported in spirit to the bedside. After some months, she referred to it in her diary as "Accompanying a dying soul," but she didn't pretend to know or understand how this wonderful errand of mercy was accomplished.

Later in February, she received a letter from her seventeen-year-old sister, Wanda. "She is begging and entreating me to help her enter the convent, She is ready for any sacrifices for God," Faustina happily noted in her diary.

Sister Faustina's time in the Pradnik sanatorium was a blessing, she came to realize. She had more time to be with Jesus. And the wonderful side effect of that was a deeper and deeper love, a greater understanding of God, more frequent occasions of mystical unity with the Lord.

On March 27, Sister Faustina returned to the convent. It was an appropriate day to go home — it was Holy Saturday, the day before Christ's Resurrection. Faustina had been elated when Dr. Silberg gave her the good news a few days earlier. At one point, he'd said that she wouldn't be released until April. No one claimed now that there had been a cure worked for Sister Faustina. The tuberculosis was too far advanced for that. But the disease was temporarily held at bay. It was as much as anyone could expect.

Reassigned to a job as gatekeeper, Sister Faustina looked forward to being useful to her congregation once again. Her new role was less physically demanding than the job as gardener. She was expected to answer the doorbell at the gate, attend to people asking for food or funds, and to take messages and packages for the convent.

But, less than two weeks after her hospital release, she was in bed again. Her coughing was violent and she felt strange pains.

On April 14, she dragged herself to Mass. After she'd received Holy Communion, she asked Jesus to send His pure and healthy blood into her own body to heal it. Within a moment of her request, she felt as though her whole body was jolted with a surge of extraordinary power and warmth. And in an instant, she felt completely well again!

Mother General Michael Moraczewska visited her sisters in Cracow near the end of the month as they renewed their vows. "Mother," Sister Faustina said to her one evening, "have you had any inspiration concerning my leaving the convent?" Naturally, Mother General had anticipated this question once again from Faustina. She knew that the issue would never be settled unless the sister — or Jesus — settled it.

The superior looked at Sister Faustina and told her that "now I leave you complete freedom to choose to do as you wish; you can leave the Congregation or you can stay."

Sister Faustina was happy with the answer and immediately planned to write to the pope to ask permission to be released from vows to her order. But once again, a cloud of sadness and reluctance overcame her, and she went back to Mother to tell her about it. This time, Mother told her that she should stay in the congregation. But she added some personal reflections. "This leaving of yours is a temptation," Mother Michael replied. "This Divine Mercy is a beautiful thing, and it must be a great work of the Lord, since Satan opposes it so much and wants to destroy it."

By the third week of May, Sister Faustina had enjoyed good health for over a month. But it suddenly occurred to her that Jesus may have preferred that she suffer in illness. "Jesus," she told Him on May 20, "do with me as You please." During the day, she began to feel the return of her illness. Her lungs felt tight and full, the coughing returned, and there were piercing pains in her abdomen. But Sister Faustina rejoiced.

It was so hot on May 22 that it was "difficult to bear," she wrote in her diary. The former gardener toured the convent gardens, noting that all the plants were wilting in the heat. Returning to her room, she decided to pray the chaplet for rain until it came. "Before supper, the sky covered over with clouds, and a heavy rain fell on the earth," she said. "I had been saying this prayer without interruption for three hours."

During the hot Cracow summer, Sister Faustina received visions of the new congregation and of the women who would be living in it. She had already written a rule for this new order. But now she was given insight about their ministries. "A member of this group ought to perform at least one act of mercy a day; at least one, but there can be many more for such deeds can easily be carried out by anyone, even the poorest," she theorized. The congregation was never far from her thoughts and earlier in the spring, she had even seen that furnishings in the house would be poor and scanty.

In late July, Sister Mary Faustina packed her bags again and moved to a tiny convent at Rabka, a mountain village south of Cracow. But the move was hardly worth the effort it cost everyone. Soon her health deteriorated once again. By the second week of August, she was back in Cracow, closer to expert medical care.

Because she had stayed such a short time in Rabka, Sister Faustina faced a barrage of questions from her sisters at Cracow. "What happened?" "Why did you come back?" "Where there problems for you at Rabka, Sister?"

Sister Faustina had less patience now for idle inquiries. In fact, she sensed that some of her sisters were asking such questions "not out of sympathy for my sufferings, but in order to add to them." Nonetheless, she dutifully explained to all that her health had become worse and that the superiors believed that she should be in Cracow, closer to her doctors.

But there was at least one sister whose harassment and opposition with regard to Faustina went beyond that of the others. She apparently disliked Sister Faustina intensely. With a gift of inner knowledge, Sister Faustina knew all about this persecutor's heart and saw her motives. She complained only to Jesus — in her diary.

"O my Jesus, when someone is unkind and unpleasant toward us, it is difficult enough to bear this kind of suffering. But this is very little in comparison to a suffering which I cannot bear; namely, that which I experience when someone exhibits kindness towards me and then lays snares at my feet at every step I take. What will power is necessary to love such a soul for God's sake."

By the middle of August, most of Sister Faustina's energies were devoted to her intercession for sinners and for the dying. On the other hand, the physical energy she needed to perform her duties as gardener was dwindling. She worked when she could.

Soon Sister Faustina turned her attentions in her diary to another matter. She wrote down the Novena to the Divine Mercy.

The words of the nine-day novena had been given to her by Jesus before Good Friday of that year. Each day of the novena, prayers were said for a different group of souls in need of God's divine mercy. When Father Sopocko visited Sister Faustina during late August, he had asked her to put the novena down on paper. Late in 1937, the novena, along with the chaplet and the litany to the Divine Mercy were published as a pamphlet under the name *"Chrystus Krol Milosierdzia"* (Christ, King of Mercy).

More and more frequently, Sister had an inner knowledge about the condition of the souls in those around her. Often, she would receive the sharp, invisible pains of the stigmata in her hands, feet, and side when she was near someone in the state of sin. But she was neither repulsed or judgmental in return. Instead, she did penance for that "certain soul."

"For sins of the flesh, I mortify the body and fast to the degree that I am permitted," she wrote. "For sins of pride, I pray with my forehead touching the floor. For sins of hatred, I pray and do some good deed for a person I find difficult. And thus I make amends according to the nature of the sin of which I am aware."

Once in mid-August, she wore a chain belt for seven hours in order to pray for a soul who had sinned in the flesh. Such "penances" were once commonly used by religious women and men. Typically, they had to receive permission for their use from a superior, as did Sister Faustina.

On August 12, the tedious sufferings and difficulties she'd experienced in recent weeks were forgotten. She was overjoyed to see her spiritual director. Father Sopocko was traveling through Cracow and stopped by for a short visit, promising to spend more time with her at the end of the month.

Two weeks later, on August 25, Father Sopocko stopped back to spend five days at the convent. It was Sister Faustina's thirty-second birthday. She had received permission to talk with him at greater length on August 29. In their conversations, Father told Sister Faustina that efforts to establish the Feast of Mercy were going well. He also told her that he was having the chaplet and the novena printed on the backs of small cards printed with the Image of Divine Mercy.

Sister Faustina listened with great interest and joy. But she could also see how much this devoted priest was suffering. His eyes were very tired, his shoulders slumped. During three Masses which he celebrated, she saw the arm of Jesus pull away from the nail on the cross. Then, light flowed from the wound of Christ to the arm of Father Sopocko, the celebrant. Sister Faustina understood that Jesus intended to strengthen Father Sopocko in the midst of the sufferings he was enduring on behalf of the Divine Mercy work.

Right after Father Sopocko's departure, Sister Faustina agonized once again over the congregation. Perhaps she felt grieved and helpless after her director's departure. He was her spiritual support, after all. Now, she saw him only rarely. She went to her diary and poured out her pain to Jesus.

Whereas she had once written about such difficulties in a stiff and stilted style, she could now freely describe and pinpoint her distress. "My fear increased when the Lord made known to me that I was to leave the Congregation. This is the third year passing by since that time, and my soul has felt, in turns, enthusiasm and an urge to act — and then I have a lot of courage and strength — and then again, when the decisive moment to undertake the work draws near, I feel deserted by God, and because of this an extraordinary fear pervades my soul, and I see that it is not the hour intended by God to initiate the work."

When would that intended hour occur? Sister Faustina knew very well that her life was like water being poured slowly out of a watering can. Soon, the container — the earthen vessel — would be empty. Then, it would be set aside. Trusting in Jesus, and remembering Father Sopocko's advice, however, she sat down one night and offered her life and sufferings once again to Jesus. She composed a lengthy "Act of Oblation." Essentially, it represented a kind of resolution to her dilemma about the new congregation. Faustina told Jesus that she would no longer agonize over the question. She would simply wait and listen.

"Bid me to stay in this convent, I will stay; bid me to undertake the work, I will undertake it; leave me in uncertainty about the work until I die, be blessed; give me death when, humanly speaking, my life seems particularly necessary, be blessed.

"From today onward, Your will, Lord, is my food. You have my whole being; dispose of me as You please. Whatever Your Fatherly hand gives me I will accept with submission, peace and joy."

These words were the final sacrifice of will, of a natural human longing to direct one's own life. Sister Faustina loved the Sisters of Our Lady of

Mercy. It was the community that Jesus had led her to as a teenager. In recent years, she had been confused and frustrated by the new direction, the "new" call she had received from the Lord. But she had listened quietly, obediently, faithfully for His directions — directions which would have taken her down a road she surely would not have chosen on her own.

But now, even that tiny remaining fiber of attachment to her community was severed. "Thy will be done," she whispered to her Lord.

Sister Faustina had a new assignment. A gardener's responsibilities were beyond her now. She no longer had the strength and energy to spend extended periods at work. On September 6, she was reassigned as gatekeeper. On the first day or two at her new post, she had to ask for help. Instead, she got scoldings for her laziness. One perturbed nun ran after Faustina into the hallway, demanding to know, "Why are you going to lie down?"

The gatekeeper's real assignment, however, had to do with suffering and prayer for sinners and the dying. On September 16, she endured terrible abdominal pains for three hours — from eight to eleven p.m. The tuberculosis which had invaded her body years before was now attacking her intestines. Sister Faustina didn't know what it was, at first. Then, she remembered that the same pains had come to her once in the sanatorium. She had told Dr. Silberg that she had never endured such horrible pains. "No medicine had an effect on me, and whatever I swallowed I threw up," she later wrote. "At times, the pain caused me to lose consciousness."

After a short time, Sister Faustina realized that she was again suffering the three-hour agony Jesus endured. She was suffering in reparation for mothers who'd aborted their unborn babies. This three-hour Calvary experience had afflicted her twice before during the same hours. At eleven p.m., the pains suddenly stopped and she fell asleep immediately, only to awaken in a very weakened state the next morning.

Three days later, Stanley Kowalski came to the convent gate and immediately recognized his sister Helena. Sister Faustina was overjoyed to see her twenty-five-year-old brother. She invited him in and soon they were seated in the convent parlor. Sister Faustina studied her brother with pride and with joy.

Stanley had grown up after she'd left home. He was a handsome, capable young man. And, she could see, that his heart was very good, loyal, and loving. Stanley told her that he wanted to enter religious life, and asked for her advice. The two of them talked about God and His goodness, but Sister Faustina was careful not to promote one religious order over another. "Surely you know best what God is asking of you," she gently told her brother, trying to encourage him to follow his heart. After they had talked some more, she embraced her brother warmly as he got up to leave. She promised him that she would ask the superior if they could talk again.

The job as gatekeeper provided Sister Faustina with a connection with the world beyond the convent which she hadn't often had. She saw more and more vividly the need for works of mercy. One day, late in September, she went to the gate and found two very poor children asking for food.

"We don't have anything to eat at home, Sister," the older child said hopefully.

Sister Faustina looked at them, wondering if that was really true. She apparently had no inner word about these youngsters. "Are you sure you have *nothing* to eat at home?" she questioned them, looking from one face to the other. The older child shrugged his shoulder, as if to shake off her accusation. But he said nothing and the two children turned away and headed down the road.

As she stared at the children's backs, Sister Faustina felt a dagger of guilt and regret in her heart. "Oh, why did I do that, Jesus?" she questioned herself. "I failed to show them Your mercy!"

Summoning up the little energy she had, the gatekeeper unlatched the gate, and started to run after the children. When they heard her calling, the children turned back and soon Sister Faustina had them seated at a table inside the convent. She gave them "as much [food] as I had permission for."

A few weeks later, a young man who was emaciated, shivering, and barefoot appeared at the main gate. It was a cold autumn day, Sister Faustina reported later in her diary. When the young man asked for something warm to eat, she hurried to the kitchen and finally found some soup. Once she'd crumpled up some bread into the soup, she gave it to him and he ate it enthusiastically. When he handed her the bowl, she saw that the young fellow was actually Jesus. He disappeared immediately, but later told her that her compassion pleased Him.

"From that moment on, there was stirred up in my heart an even purer love toward the poor and the needy," the gatekeeper wrote that evening. "Oh, how happy I am that my superiors have given me such a task! I understand that mercy is manifold, one can do good always and everywhere and at all times. An ardent love of God sees all around itself constant opportunities to share itself through deed, word and prayer."

Occasionally, the same poor people came repeatedly to the convent gate for food. Whenever Sister Faustina noticed that they'd been there before, she treated the visitors with even greater kindness. But not everyone agreed with her open-handed approach.

"One should not deal with beggars in this way," Faustina's assistant told her one day, when she observed Faustina doling out food to "repeaters." But the poor saw a welcoming and non-judgmental spirit in Sister Faustina. She tried to break through the humiliation she often saw in their eyes and often, they spoke with her more freely. Over a bowl of soup, a bond of friendship sometimes formed.

Near the end of September, Sister Faustina and Mother Irene traveled into Cracow. They wanted to double-check the printing of the Divine Mercy holy cards and chaplets. Father Sopocko's booklet was called "Christ, King of Mercy." The Lord let the gatekeeper know that the cards and chaplets would help in the salvation of many people. She rejoiced in the news and also in the constant and loving assistance of her supportive Mother Superior.

On the tenth of October, Sister Faustina received a new message from Jesus about the Divine Mercy prayers. Jesus said that three o'clock was "the hour of great mercy." Identifying herself with Him at that hour of the day meant a more intimate link with Christ's Passion and His abandonment. The Lord promised Faustina that He would "refuse nothing to the soul that makes a request of Me in virtue of My Passion."

This new instruction about "the hour of great mercy" was the final addition to the Mercy devotions. First, on February 22, 1931, she had received the vision of the Divine Mercy image. On that same day in 1931, Jesus also asked for a Feast of Mercy to be celebrated on the First Sunday after Easter. Then, on September 13, 1935, Faustina received the prayers which comprised the Chaplet of Divine Mercy. On Good Friday, 1937, the Lord dictated the intentions for the nine-day Novena of Divine Mercy which utilized the chaplet.

And so now, with this new devotion, the frail but faithful "Apostle of Divine Mercy" began to pray the Chaplet each day at three o'clock. Sometimes, she was at the gate. Sometimes, she was busy with sewing or helping a bit in the kitchen. But, to a lesser or greater degree, from then on, she always devoted her attention to prayer during the "hour of great mercy." When she could go to chapel, she stretched out on the floor and prayed with arms outstretched, her body forming the shape of a cross.

During the annual eight-day retreat later on in October, Sister Faustina was acutely aware that it would be her last one. Jesus assured her that her efforts to become a saint would be rewarded through her persistence. Later, Sister Faustina wrote about this lifelong desire. There was little time left for poetic allusions and innuendo. She wanted to be very direct with her Lord.

"My Jesus, You know that from my earliest years I have wanted to become a great saint; that is to say, I have wanted to love You with a love so great that there would be no soul who has hitherto loved You so. At first these desires of mine were kept secret, and only Jesus knew of them. But today I cannot contain them within my heart; I would like to cry out to the whole world, 'Love God, because He is good and great is His mercy!' "

As the weeks of winter went by, she grew weaker and weaker. As she made her way down the convent corridors, she had to stop often to lean against the wall to catch her breath or wait for the end of a coughing spell. Moving up and down the stairs was agonizing. And sometimes, she simply didn't have the strength to get up out of bed.

It was time to give way, to give in to death and disintegration. And heaven began to remind her of this in the most painful and humbling ways. She seemed to be subjected to every humiliation, every form of torture that nature could concoct. Her diary was becoming a chronicle of the sad but redemptive destruction of a young woman's life.

"One day, I began to doubt as to how it was possible to feel this continual decaying of the body and at the same time to be able to walk and work. Perhaps this was some kind of an illusion. Yet it cannot be an illusion, because it causes me such terrible pains. As I was thinking about this, one of the sisters came to converse with me. After a minute or two, she made a terribly wry face and said, 'Sister, I smell a corpse here, as though it were all decaying. Oh, how dreadful it is!' I said to her, 'Don't be frightened, Sister, that smell of a corpse comes from me.' She was very surprised and said that she could not stand it any longer. After she had gone, I understood that God had allowed her to sense this so that I would have no doubt, but that He was no less than miraculously keeping the knowledge of this suffering from the whole community."

God was allowing even the decomposition of her body before actual death! Though saddened, she did not object. She saw that God wanted her to let go of everything — everything but her desire to suffer as Jesus did.

In late November, she joyfully opened a letter from Father Sopocko. He told her that God was demanding prayer and sacrifice and not action on behalf of the new community. Sister Faustina understood and she nodded her head in agreement as she reread his counsels. On the last day of November, in the evening, she was praying in her cell. In just a few moments, she rediscovered how much Satan wanted to prevent her from offering up her sufferings.

Instantaneously, she was overcome by a distaste for everything having to do with God. Then, she heard Satan say, "Think no more about this work. God is not as merciful as you say He is. Do not pray for sinners, because they will be damned all the same, and by this work of mercy you expose your own self to damnation. Talk no more about this mercy of God with your confessor and especially not with Father Sopocko and Father Andrasz."

Suddenly, Sister Faustina whirled around. She saw that the voice was coming from the figure of her guardian angel. And yet — she knew that this was not her guardian angel. "I know who you are: the father of lies," she said quietly but firmly, as she made the sign of the cross. The angel flew into a hideous rage and disappeared.

A few weeks later, she prepared her heart to celebrate her last Christmas on earth. At the Christmas Midnight Mass, Sister Faustina had a vision of the little stable at Bethlehem. She saw the Blessed Virgin wrapping the newborn Jesus in swaddling clothes as Joseph slept on the hay. When the child was placed in the manger, Joseph woke up and began to pray. Then, Faustina found herself alone with the child. He awoke and stretched out His hands to her. When she picked Him up and held Him next to her heart, she knew that He was happy, content. Then, the vision faded with the Communion bell.

Towards the end of Mass, a wave of nausea and pain swept over her. Feeling so ill on this Christmas Eve, the pale sister made her way out of the chapel and struggled up the stairs. She knew what her "gifts" were on this Christmas night. Jesus had appeared as a precious newborn. But now, she was also being given the privilege of suffering with Him.

Having reached the top of the steps, Sister Faustina sighed and stopped for a second to catch her breath. Up the stairs drifted the sweet strains of a Christmas carol being sung by her sisters in the chapel below. Painfully, she made her way to bed, smiling at the thought of a tiny Jesus asleep in straw.

14

Apostle of Mercy

May Your grace, which flows down upon me from Your Compassionate Heart, strengthen me for the struggle and sufferings, that I may remain faithful to You. And although I am such misery, I do not fear You, because I know Your mercy well. Nothing will frighten me away from You, O God, because everything is so much less than what I know Your mercy to be — **Diary, 1803**.

"I am ending the old year with suffering and beginning the new one with suffering as well." That's what Sister Faustina wrote in her diary on January 1, 1938 — the first day of the last year of her earthly life. She wasn't yielding to a maudlin depression. She was merely stating the state of affairs. The last cruel stages of her illness — her journey up to Calvary — had begun.

A violent cough rarely left her now. Cramping pains in her intestines and nausea had been added to the coughing. And the result of it all was exhaustion, and a sense of isolation in her infirmary room.

"Sister, why didn't you go to Mass?" the infirmarian, Sister Chrysostom, wanted to know on the morning of January 1, a feast day. When Sister Faustina wearily tried to explain that she had been too ill to get out of bed, Sister Chrysostom merely clucked her disapproval and left. She had many patients to care for, and she hadn't been in to check on Faustina for two days.

And when a sister assigned to the kitchen wondered why Sister Faustina hadn't been to the kitchen to get the buttermilk ordered for her, the exhausted patient simply sighed and said, "There was no one to bring it to me."

"Welcome, New Year. Welcome, cup of bitterness," she wrote in her New Year's Day entry.

On the other hand, Sister Faustina knew very well that after her approaching Good Friday, there would be new life and Resurrection. Her tired and diseased body would be renewed and healthy again. Her sad moments and isolation would be replaced by unfading joy. And when the weariness of her long illness oppressed her, she reminded herself of these things.

Sister was given the inner knowledge that several of her sisters were praying for her. In particular, she understood that Mother Irene often asked for God's blessings on her and on the Divine Mercy efforts. But the rejection she felt from some of the other sisters still wounded her. By nature, she was a sociable person. She'd come from a close and loving family and had chosen this congregation as her new family. Emotionally, she now needed the loving support from this family. Because of her isolating illness and possible misunderstandings, it wasn't being given to her.

After a night of pain and loneliness, she wrote that "when the chaplain brought me Holy Communion, I had to control myself by sheer effort of will to keep from crying out at the top of my voice, 'Welcome, my true and only Friend.'"

Faustina was an emotional person, but now, she was especially so, deeply fragile and vulnerable. Between the bouts of nausea and pain, she was often on the verge of tears. For a week or so, she had put off asking Father Andrasz to hear her confession. She was afraid that she would break down in tears. Then, Jesus corrected her and she thankfully received the sacrament.

Sister Mary Faustina understood that this abandonment was part of the suffering that Jesus wanted her to accept. And she did accept it. But, she was still hurt when the infirmarian berated her for "giving in to weakness." Perhaps the infirmarian was trying to encourage Faustina to fight the disease, but the ailing sister wasn't given any rationales for the tough treatment. The sister designated to clean Faustina's room was deathly afraid of tuberculosis and didn't come for weeks at a time.

One night, as she was struggling to make her way back to her cell, she was met by the Sister Assistant, who wanted one of the nuns to go out in the pouring rain to the gate with a message for someone. When she spotted Sister Faustina, a member of the second choir, she told Faustina to do the errand. "I answered, 'All right,' and went and carried out the order, but only God knows the whole of it," remembered a wounded Sister Faustina.

"Sometimes it would seem that a sister of the second choir is made of stone, but she is also human and has a heart and feelings," she wrote, emptying her feelings onto the pages of her diary.

Still, in January, she found the strength to write and write and write. Jesus had told her to spend all of her free time writing. She wrote a series of conversations between Jesus, the Merciful God, and different souls — the sinful soul, the despairing soul, a suffering soul, a soul striving for perfection, and a perfect soul (*Diary*, 1485-1490). The conversations were a summary of many of the theological truths that Sister Faustina had come to understand.

By the end of that month, she was able to return to the dining room to share meals with her sisters. But she was certainly not strong enough to return to her duties as gatekeeper. Instead, during the day she remained in her cell, crocheting lace for the altar cloths. "I enjoy this work very much," she wrote, "but still, even with such light work, I tire easily. I see how feeble I am."

Once again, she had regained an equilibrium about her sufferings. Life was not quite so bleak. Perhaps she really had needed to rejoin her sisters — at least for meals. "If not in one way, then in another, I glorify God; and if God were to give me a second life, I do not know whether I would make better use of it," she wrote.

Naturally, she wondered how long she had to live. She knew that it would be less than a year. She told Jesus, "You make many secrets known to me; but that one secret — the hour of my death — You do not want to tell me." But Jesus did not tell her yet. "Be at peace," He advised. "I will let you know, but not just now."

She was at peace often when she worked at the handloom in her room. It was used to make lace to edge altar linens. She enjoyed this handiwork, and sometimes she found herself in the middle of a wonderful daydream. Sometimes, Sister Faustina would "go" home to Glogowiec.

Once again, she was walking up through her father's pasture with Genevieve, Josephine, and a few of the little ones. They were going to fetch the cows but there was no hurry. The morning's summer sun was very warm, and the sweet smell of wild flowers filled their nostrils. There was time to lie in the grass in the shade and sing songs with her sisters and little brothers. Josephine had brought some bread and a bit of cheese for a noonday snack. The little ones in the family had brought a ball and some small hand-carved wooden toys to play with in the tall grass. "I will never forget the way the meadow grass feels when you're barefoot," the thin-faced sister smiled and said to herself. But such journeys to the past disappeared as quickly as they came. With a slight shake of her head, the busy sister was returned fully to her sick-room.

In fact, nobody at home in Glogowiec really realized how ill their Helena was. Sister Faustina had some contact with her parents and her siblings, but not very much. She thought of them often and wondered how her parents were.

Spiritual struggles plagued her during February. She endured terrible temptations to despair and disbelief. She weathered them, although she feared that even her confessor, Father Andrasz, wouldn't understand her. Preferring to suffer in silence was a mistake. The decision lengthened her suffering, and Jesus soon criticized her lack of humility and obedience. "From the moment I gave you this priest as spiritual director, I endowed him with new light so that he might easily know and understand your soul," Jesus informed her. Soon, she went to confession and confessed her faults with great humility.

After February 3, Sister Faustina did not date the entries of her diary. Perhaps, it was a sign of growing fatigue — or an understanding that there was no longer any need to keep track of her days.

Early in February, while she was writing in her cell, Satan stood nearby, banging things, trying to disrupt and distract her. She continued writing, trying to ignore the noise. A few days later, she received a message which reminded her again of her mission of mercy. "Today I am sending you with My mercy to the whole of mankind. I do not want to punish aching mankind, but I desire to heal it, pressing it to My merciful Heart. Before the Day of Justice I am sending the Day of Mercy."

A week or two later, Sister Faustina went to visit some of the sisters in the convent infirmary. They were ill with the flu. One of the sisters told Faustina quite frankly that she wanted her to visit her after her death! This sister wanted to share a secret about her soul and asked Sister Faustina to settle the matter with Jesus since she would soon be in heaven. It was already assumed by many of Faustina's sisters that she was close to death *and* close to Jesus.

Surprised, Sister Faustina hedged. She didn't want the other nun to discuss personal matters publicly. "The Lord Jesus is very discreet," Sister Faustina told her gently. "And so He never betrays to anyone a secret that is between Him and a soul." But very soon, there were other sisters who began to visit or write to Sister Faustina. Though she had so often been misunderstood and mistreated by many of her peers, many Sisters of Our Lady of Mercy also recognized a holiness in her. And since her life was clearly coming to an end, sisters from both the first and second choirs wanted to connect with that undeniable holiness.

By March, Sister Faustina's intestinal pains had become so intense that she often fainted during an attack. The convent doctor could find no cause for them, and even Mother Irene told Faustina that it was a lack of charity to disturb her sleeping sisters with her groans of pain at night.

In fact, the tuberculosis infection had reached her intestines. The tubercular foci had spread all over the intestines. About two hours after eating, when the food reached the intestines, Sister Faustina was stricken with excruciating pain, a pain that could only be controlled by the strongest pain medications. Dr. Silberg was called in again to see what he would advise. And Sister Faustina soon learned that she would undergo more treatments at the sanatorium.

On March 25, Jesus appeared. Sister Faustina saw that He was suffering terribly. When He asked her if she would join him to "help me to save sinners," she readily agreed. Within a week, burning fevers were added to her agonizing list of ailments. She could no longer eat solid foods and was therefore constantly aching for something refreshing to drink. Somehow, her constant requests were frequently ignored or forgotten. Like Jesus on the cross, she was thirsty but received no satisfying drink.

In other ways, too, she was the victim of surprising neglect. Since she was increasingly confined to bed, she could do less and less for herself. And often, no one even came to light a fire in the stove to warm her room. It was early spring and the cold drafts only made her cough worse.

On the first Friday of April, she was weaker still. Someone had handed her a copy of a magazine, *The Messenger of the Sacred Heart*. In it, she read the article about the canonization of St. Andrew Bobola, a seventeenth-century martyred Polish Jesuit from Vilnius. He had worked for the return of Orthodox Christians to union with Rome. The power of the saint's witness touched her, and she began to weep.

She said to Jesus, "I know Your generosity, and yet it seems to me that You are less generous toward us." There was no canonized saint in her congregation. "Don't cry," Jesus responded. "You are that saint."

Much of the time now, Sister Faustina was confined to her bed. Since she was not able to eat, she was becoming very thin and gaunt. On Holy Thursday, April 14, however, she felt strong enough to participate in the services. Jesus asked her to "Look, and enter into My Passion." In just an instant, she relived the entire Passion of the Lord in her own heart. "I was surprised," she wrote later, "that these tortures did not deprive me of my life."

On Good Friday, Jesus appeared and said to her, "You are My Heart. Speak to sinners about My mercy." And on the following day, when the Church was quiet, waiting for the triumph of the Resurrection, Jesus reassured her that she had indeed been obedient, carrying out His will, just as He had told her to do it.

On Easter, Sister Faustina had the strength to participate in the procession, but only because she had begged Jesus to fortify her. As she stood in line with the other sisters, He appeared, shining as brightly as the sun. Her soul was immersed in the Lord in ecstasy and when she came to herself again, she was walking along in procession with the other sisters.

Two days after Easter, Sister Faustina was able to go to recreation with her sisters. A discussion about her took place immediately. It didn't seem to matter to the other nuns that the sister in question — the subject of discussion — sat quietly in their midst. Viewing the experience with some wry detachment, Sister Faustina later reported it in her diary.

Sister Cajetan opened a discussion of Faustina's approaching death by declaring confidently, "Sister Faustina is doing so poorly that she can hardly walk, but may she die soon because she is going to be a saint." Then, as Sister Faustina noted, one of the directresses, Sister Casimir, corrected Cajetan by noting that "whether she is going to be a saint, that is another question." Then, as Sister Faustina recalled, there began "some malicious remarks on the subject. I kept silent; then I put in a word, but I saw that the conversation was getting worse, so again I fell silent."

On April 21, Sister Faustina was back at Pradnik for further treatment. Dr. Silberg had suggested that she should remain at the sanatorium for two months or longer. Sister Faustina had worried that she might be put in a noisy ward. She prayed for a private one and was very happy when she was given one.

When the sister who was her nurse told her that she would not receive the Eucharist on the following days because she would be too tired, Faustina was deeply hurt. This, after all, was her food, her strength. Instead, a seraph — an angel — appeared and gave her Holy Communion. According to her diary, "this was repeated for thirteen days, although I was never sure that he would bring me Holy Communion the next day."

During the evening of May 1, Jesus asked Sister Faustina, "My daughter, do you need anything?" "O my Love, when I have You I have everything," she answered. Then, Jesus asked her to continue to write about His mercy so that souls would let Him sanctify and fulfill them. His counseling continued. Jesus was her spiritual director now. He was preparing her for her final days, the days when the agony of her passing would intensify.

"Do not ask for anything without consulting Me," He cautioned her. "Allow them to take away even what is due you — respect, your good name — let your spirit rise above all that. And so, set free from everything, rest close to My Heart, not allowing your peace to be disturbed by anything."

Jesus even guided her in her work with the diary. He urged her to focus on His Divine Mercy. "Your task is to write down everything that I make known to you about My mercy, for the benefit of those who by reading these things will be comforted in their souls and will have the courage to approach Me. I therefore want you to devote all you free moments to writing."

Sister Faustina undoubtedly felt pressured by this command. She felt terribly weak and ill, and the entries in her diary became less focused. But she was obedient. She prayed. In spirit, she accompanied and interceded for dying souls and those already in purgatory. And, she wrote.

One day after Communion, Jesus told her, "If you did not tie My hands, I would send down many punishments upon the earth. My daughter, your look disarms My anger." Near the end of May, she awoke in the middle of the night during a violent storm. "Say the chaplet I have taught you, and the storm will cease," she was told. Soon after she had begun the prayer, the storm ceased. "Through the chaplet you will obtain everything, if what you ask for will be compatible with My will," Jesus told her.

On June 2, Sister Faustina began a three-day retreat in the sanatorium. Jesus was her Retreat Master! He "preached" her conferences and told her what Scripture readings He wanted her to read each day. The readings were John 15, 19, and 21. On Pentecost Sunday, she rose early and went to the chapel. She was excited about the idea of renewing her vows on this day. After Holy Communion, "His breath filled my soul with such delight," she wrote.

On June 17, a Friday, she was sure that she was dying. She was feverish and vomited blood during the night. It felt to her as though her entire body was dying. When she recovered once again, she told Jesus, "You are fooling me, Jesus; You show me the open gate of heaven, but again You leave me on earth." But the Lord consoled her and told her that He understood her longing for heaven.

Sometime late in June, Sister Faustina stopped writing in her diary. She no longer had the strength to hold the pen. Her last entry concluded with the words which fittingly summarized her life, her courage, and her persistence in suffering.

"May your grace, which flows down upon me from Your Compassionate Heart, strengthen me for the struggle and sufferings, that I may remain faithful to You. And although I am such misery, I do not fear You, because I know Your mercy well. Nothing will frighten me away from You, O God, because everything is so much less than what I know [your mercy to be] — I see that clearly."

In four years, she had written in six notebooks the equivalent of four hundred seventy-seven printed pages.

In July, Mother Michael, the Mother General of the congregation, visited Sister Faustina at the sanatorium. It was a tender, loving visit and Faustina talked about various things that had happened to her at the hospital. They both knew that they wouldn't meet again. "Oh, Mother, what beautiful things Jesus is telling me!" the dying nun told Mother Michael before she left.

In August, Mother received a phone call, telling her that Sister Faustina was failing. She wrote a personal letter, assuring her of her prayers and love. Mother Michael also told Sister that Father Sopocko would undoubtedly visit her soon. He was attending a synod at Czestochowa. Sister Faustina was delighted to hear that, and when she had sufficient strength, she wrote a letter in return to her Mother General.

"Dearest Mother," Sister Faustina wrote, "it seems to me that this is our last conversation on earth. I am very weak, and am writing with trembling hand." Sister Faustina thanked Mother Michael for her compassion and direction in her religious life. Then, she asked for her forgiveness for her faults and for any troubles in her religious life.

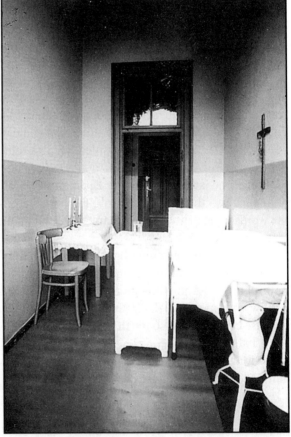

© **Marians of the Immaculate Conception**

"Good-bye, Dearest Mother," she concluded, "we shall see each other in heaven at the foot of God's throne. And now, may The Divine Mercy be glorified in us and through us." She signed her letter, "The greatest misery and nothingness, Sister Faustina."

On August 25, Sister Faustina's thirty-third birthday, she was sinking ever closer to death. Father Czaputa, the chaplain of the convent, came to administer the Sacrament of the Anointing of the Sick. About a week later, Father Sopocko visited her, encouraging her and

The cell in the infirmary of the convent in Cracow-Lagiewniki where Faustina died on October 5, 1938.

praying with her. After he left, he realized that he had forgotten to give Sister Faustina some newly printed prayer-cards. When he returned to her room, he found her alone in her room in ecstasy. He didn't disturb her; she was coming closer and closer to her Lord.

Sister Faustina wanted to die at home — in the convent. On September 17, Sister Alfreda, a new infirmarian, arrived at the sanatorium to bring her back. Dr. Silberg stopped by her room and asked to keep the little holy card of St. Thérèse which had been on the night table near Faustina's bed. He wanted to hang it above the bed of his little six-year-old son. Sister Faustina smiled and gave it to the doctor, who had often come to discuss theological matters with her. Then, Sister Alfreda and her fragile patient made their way home.

Back at St. Joseph's Convent, Sister Faustina was helped up to bed. She was given a private room in the infirmary wing. A narrow, austere room with high ceilings, her last bedroom was sparsely furnished. But very little was needed now. There was an iron bed, a night stand, and a chair or two for visitors. A large crucifix hung on the wall, about a foot-and-a-half above her head.

Twenty-seven-year-old Sister Amelia Socha, a close friend of Sister Faustina's, was on hand to take care of her. And since Amelia also had tuberculosis in her hands, she wasn't endangering herself by giving loving attention to the infectious patient.

Because Sister Faustina could no longer eat, there was less to do for her. She was, however, often thirsty and needed fluids. Dark circles appeared beneath those gray-green eyes. Her cheeks were sunken, and her whole face had become skeletal in appearance. And yet, there was a patient joy, a profound happiness in her.

On September 22, Sister Faustina asked pardon from her entire community for her shortcomings. She knew that she would soon be too weak to do it. On the twenty-sixth, Father Sopocko returned to see her and found that she was again speaking intimately with God.

"She gives the impression of an unearthly being," he wrote in his memoirs later. "I no longer have the least doubt that what is found in her diary, concerning Holy Communion being administered to her by an Angel is true." As Father Sopocko spoke a few final words to his dying friend, she told him the date of her approaching death. Jesus had finally revealed it to her — October 5.

Mother Irene, the superior, looked in on her frequently. She saw that Sister Faustina was now very peaceful and calm. Mother remembered the many conversations she had had with this dying nun. Faustina had been frantic and distressed that the work of Divine Mercy was not going well. But now, she was resigned, leaving everything in God's good hands.

A day or two before her death, Sister Faustina had a secret to share with Mother Irene. The dying young sister beckoned her superior to come closer to her bed. "The Lord Jesus wants to elevate me and make me a saint," she whispered. Mother Irene was profoundly touched by the message but also by the way that Sister Faustina had told her this — "without a shade of pride. When I left Sister, I was strangely moved by the remark, but not fully aware of the importance of these words," she said later.

On October 5, Sister Faustina whispered to Sister Felicia, "Today, the Lord is taking me." At four p.m., Father Andrasz came to hear Faustina's last confession. She was suffering immensely with her pains. She asked for an injection, but when the infirmarian arrived, the suffering sister decided to forgo it. She still wanted to suffer whatever God would send to her.

In the evening, the sisters gathered around Sister Faustina's bed with the chaplain and prayed with her. She was still conscious, but it seemed as if the end was near. Father Czaputa led the prayers for the dying. The sisters added the prayer, "O, Most Kind Jesus."

Then, they recited Psalm 130. "Out of the depths I cry to you, O Lord; Lord, hear my voice." The Sisters of Our Lady of Mercy intoned the psalm slowly and reverently as they watched the labored breathing of their Sister Faustina.

"Let your ears be attentive to my voice in supplication. If you, O Lord, mark iniquities, Lord, who can stand? But with you is forgiveness, that you may be revered. I trust in the Lord; my soul trusts in his word. My soul waits for the Lord more than sentinels wait for the dawn."

These ancient words about the mercy of the Lord were among the last sounds that Sister Faustina heard on earth. And when the sisters left the room soon after the prayers were completed, Sister Faustina's breathing became more shallow. At 10:45 p.m., she quietly exhaled one more time and then stopped breathing. Her death was so peaceful that when Sister Liguoria ran to get Mother Irene, the Apostle of the Divine Mercy was already in the waiting arms of her Lord.

Sister Liguoria, Sister Eufemia Traczynska, and Mother Irene stood a few moments later, gazing at the body of Sister Faustina. They were stunned. She was lovely again. The pinched look from the agonies she had endured was fading. Her expression was relaxed, and there was just the hint of a smile upon her face.

Mother Irene stood for a few more moments, gazing at the remarkable young sister, fingering her rosary in her pocket. She knelt by the bed again, and prayed for her. She thought about the many conversations she had had with Sister Faustina about God's wonderful mercy. Sister Faustina had always insisted that God is Love and Mercy itself. And at this moment, Mother Irene Krzyzanowska had the idea that this sister from the second choir would continue to share that Good News for a very long time to come.

"We will have her funeral on Friday," Mother told the sisters, finally breaking the silence. "It will be October 7, the Feast of Our Lady of the Rosary. Sister Faustina will be happy about that. Now, I must go and phone Mother General."

15

A Movement of Divine Mercy

*Today, I want to be transformed, whole and entire, into the love of Jesus and to offer myself, together with Him, to the Heavenly Father — **Diary, 1820**.*

The Sisters of Our Lady of Mercy quickly wrote Sister Faustina's family in Glogowiec to tell of her death. There had never been a phone in the family home. The sisters shared the edifying story of Sister Faustina's final illness and holy death. The congregation, Faustina's second family, sent condolences and prayers to the large and loving Kowalski family into which she'd been born.

Seventy-year-old Stanislaus Kowalski and sixty-three-year-old Marianna Kowalska were heartbroken. Tears streamed down their faces. Bent and worn-out by their many years of grueling labor, they were still very poor. God had indeed blessed them with many children. But their favorite child, the one they had tried so hard to keep nearby, was gone. Sister Faustina — their Helena — was just thirty-three years old.

Stanislaus stared at his own wrinkled hands until his eyes brimmed with tears again. He wondered why the Creator hadn't reached for his hands instead. His daughter was so good, so beautiful in every way. Didn't the world desperately need such souls?

In fact, Sister Faustina had told her superiors that she didn't want her family to hear any unnecessary details of her terminal illness or even about her death right away. None of them had visited her during her last days. No family members attended her funeral. They were so poor. Traveling to Cracow would have been a great hardship — financially and emotionally. She also knew that seeing her gaunt and ravaged body — as well as her excruciating suffering — would have grieved them so much. She knew her family well. There would be enough pain for them without witnessing her death.

Sister Faustina's family soon consoled themselves somewhat with the memories of her visit home in 1935. Then — at least, for a few days — she had belonged to them once again. Faustina's father, who had always been a storyteller, now told his stories about Helena over and over. They brought her back to him. It was a connection — at least for a little while.

But within a year of her death, many of the Sisters of Our Lady of Mercy were also thinking a lot about what Sister Faustina had said and done. They often visited the place where she was buried in the common community grave in Lagiewniki. They remembered that she often begged them to pray with her for Poland. She had predicted that their homeland would suffer terribly. "There will be a war — a terrible, terrible war," she said many times, often covering her eyes as though to shield herself from visions of the horrors.

The dreadful prophecy came true. In August of 1939, Germany and the USSR had secretly agreed to divide up Poland again. On September 1, 1939, Germany invaded Poland, and World War II began. Tanks and troops stormed through the country which had been conquered so many times in its troubled history. On September 17, the USSR invaded Poland from the east. By 1941, Germany occupied all of Poland, destroying much of it in an effort to push back the Russians. Warsaw, the

Sister Irene Krzyzanowska, Faustina's superior in Vilnius and Cracow during the last years of her life.

Polish capital, was almost completely destroyed, although Cracow remained untouched.

Sister Faustina had foreseen that. She had also predicted that her sisters in Cracow would be threatened many times but would never have to abandon their convent. Mother Irene Krzyzanowska, the superior at Cracow, later recalled, "On three occasions, there was a direct danger of being thrown out by the Germans. All the sisters went to the grave of Sister Faustina to pray for her intercessions to the Divine Mercy that we be left in peace. Each time the danger passed, and we did not leave our house throughout the war."

The war tore the close-knit Kowalski family apart. In 1939, twenty-five-year-old Mecislaus was drafted into the Polish army and spent most of the war in a German prisoner-of-war camp. Marianna Lucyna and Wanda Kowalska — as well as Eugeniusz Olszynski, husband of Natalia — were taken to work camps in Germany. Eugeniusz died there.

Soon after the war broke out, the sisters in Cracow opened their private chapel to the public. If this was not the right time to plead for God's mercy, there never would be one. People began to visit the chapel and the tomb of Sister Faustina. They had heard that she was a devotee of God's divine mercy. Polish pilgrims came to the convent to get holy cards, novenas, and chaplets.

Even before Sister Faustina died, Mother Irene had hung a print of the Merciful Jesus above the St. Joseph altar. Copies of the Divine Mercy prayers and image were carried in small pamphlets which Father Sopocko had printed. They were stuffed into pockets and carried everywhere, even outside the country, as Poles began to scatter, trying to escape imprisonment and the war. Poland desperately needed the Lord's mercy and began to pray hard for it.

In 1943, an artist named Adolph Hyla painted a new version of Jesus of the Divine Mercy. Hyla donated it to the convent at Cracow as a sort of votive offering for his family's safety during the war. It was considerably larger than the original image painted by Kazimierowski still hanging in St. Michael's Church in Vilnius. The Hyla portrait was placed above a side altar in Cracow. Immediately, this second version of the Merciful Jesus became very popular. Many candles were constantly lit near it.

As images of the Merciful Jesus were obtained by churches, they were often ceremoniously enthroned. With permission from the dioceses, different communities and parishes celebrated the Feast of Divine Mercy on "Low Sunday," or the "First Sunday after Easter."

Before and during the war, the devotions had their largest followings in Vilnius and in Cracow. In Vilnius, international politics favored the spread of the Divine Mercy devotions in a unique way. Before World War II, the city was a part of Poland. In 1939, as the war broke out, the Soviet Union occupied Vilnius in an attempt to claim portions of Poland.

When Archbishop Romuald Jalbrzykowski, the archbishop of Vilnius, and a friend of Sister Faustina's, saw that her predictions about the war were coming true, he permitted the story about the Kazimierowski painting to be released. Once the "secret" was made public, great crowds visited and venerated the image. The Divine Mercy prayers and devotions were also printed and distributed there.

When Mother General Michael Moraczewska heard about the huge success of the Divine Mercy devotions in Vilnius, she decided to tell all of her sisters about its connection with their own Sister Mary Faustina. Sister Faustina had not spoken to the sisters about her mission, but had spoken of it only to her superiors. The time was right, and the nation clearly needed the spiritual support that prayer for mercy could bring. Mother Michael also finally believed that all of the Sisters of Our Lady of Mercy should know about this movement. Indeed, Sister Faustina's apostolate on behalf of the Divine Mercy echoed the foundational spirituality of the congregation.

When her sisters began to read parts of her diary soon after her death, they discovered a strange prediction she'd made in 1935. It dealt with the Divine Mercy devotions. Sister Faustina said that the Mercy message would be suppressed for a while. She also said that her spiritual director, Father Michael Sopocko, would endure terrible anguish because of his close association with the message.

"There will come a time," she said, "when this work, which God is demanding so very much, will be as though utterly undone. And then God will act with great power, which will give evidence of its authenticity. It will be a new splendor for the Church, although it has been dormant in it from long ago. That God is merciful, no one can deny. He desires everyone to know this before He comes again as Judge."

After the war, the natural rhythms of life were mended very slowly in Poland. The Kowalski family was no different from many others.

Neither Wanda nor young Stanley was able to follow the dream to enter religious life. While interred in a German work camp, Wanda met and married an Englishman, and settled in England after the war. After her husband died, she tried to return to Poland, but was refused by the country's Communist rulers. Stanley became a carpenter like his father. He married and worked as a church organist in Lodz.

Marianna Lucyna, who had also been interred in a German work camp, returned to Poland after the war. She became a railway conductor and died after an accident on the railway in 1956. Natalia, whose husband Eugeniusz Olszynski had died in Germany, married a second time in Lodz.

By the early 1950s, it didn't seem as though Sister Faustina's prediction of suppression would come true. By 1951 — thirteen years after the death of Sister Faustina — there were one hundred thirty Divine Mercy Centers in her homeland.

However, according to the Postulator of the Faustina Cause, there was a problem with the Divine Mercy's rapid acceptance. "This was the fact that the devotion was based almost exclusively on the revelations made by Our Lord Jesus Christ to Sister Faustina, — private revelations and on forms [of devotion] inspired by her. The devotion needed a solid scriptural and theological base."

Father Sopocko and a few others had started to explore the Divine Mercy message theologically. There was no doubt about the fact that Scripture was filled with references to the "unfathomable mercy of God," as Sister Faustina often referred to it. And several renowned scholars carefully established the claim that mercy was God's greatest attribute. But there hadn't been time to do all the needed research and writing before the Sacred Congregation for the Doctrine of the Faith examined the Divine Mercy devotions. Unfortunately, the Sacred Congregation worked with a French translation of the diary, which had been poorly done. And there were other reasons for confusion about her work.

Sister Faustina's education was flawed, says Father Seraphim Michalenko, M.I.C., Vice-Postulator of Blessed Faustina's canonization cause. Her spelling was not good and she had never been instructed in the proper use of punctuation. And so, when Sister wrote out the messages from Jesus, she used no quotation marks. It was easy to assume that some of the messages she was attributing to Jesus, Mary, and some of the saints were her own words. When read in that light, Sister Faustina seemed to be guilty of religious fanaticism or even blasphemy.

As a result, the Vatican theologians initially received a very poor impression of the message Sister Faustina worked so hard to share with the world. On March 6, 1959, the Holy See prohibited the spread of all of the Divine Mercy devotions.

After the ban, the Divine Mercy images were removed from many churches. Priests no longer preached about the Divine Mercy of God on the Second Sunday of Easter. Father Sopocko was severely admonished by the Holy See for his role in promoting the Divine Mercy devotions. For a theologian who had diligently devoted his life to the Church, this was a heavy blow.

In Cracow, the Sisters of Our Lady of Mercy were told not to distribute the holy cards and prayer pamphlets any longer. Because the image of the Divine Mercy at their side altar was already venerated by many people in Cracow, the sisters were allowed to keep that. The archbishop of Cracow also permitted the sisters to continue the celebrations and devotions that were popular there. Other than that, however, the movement went no further.

Five years after the ban, in 1964, the newly appointed archbishop of Cracow, Archbishop Karol Wojtyla, discussed the possibilities of investigating the life and virtues of Sister Faustina Kowalska. Better than anyone else, he knew that the people of his diocese already believed that she was a saint.

Cardinal Ottaviani, the Secretary of the Sacred Congregation, urged the archbishop to open an investigation quickly — before all the witnesses to Faustina's life were dead. The ban on the Divine Mercy devotions did not mean that Sister Faustina herself was not a saint.

Eagerly, Archbishop Wojtyla returned to Cracow and opened the investigation of Sister Faustina's life in the autumn of 1965. For two years, the diocesan commission gathered all the information available about this sister who had died twenty-seven years earlier. The researchers collected documents, letters, testimonies, photos, personal effects. Many of her family members were still living. Her mother, Marianna Kowalska, lived until the age of ninety. She died in 1965 and was buried near her husband and their babies in the Kowalski section of the cemetery of Swinice.

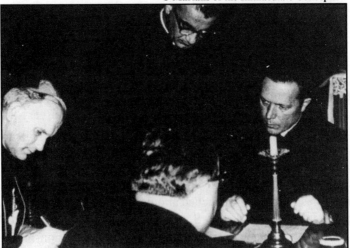

Karol Cardinal Wojtyla, later Pope John Paul II, signing documents at the close of the diocesan informational process towards Sister Faustina's beatification on September 20, 1967.

Then one day in September of 1967, the fruits of this investigation were boxed and sent to the Sacred Congregation for the Causes of Saints in Rome. The congregation approved the case, and the inauguration for Sister Faustina's beatification cause began in 1968.

In 1977, Cardinal Wojtyla asked the Sacred Congregation for the Doctrine of the Faith to review the ban on the Divine Mercy devotions. It had been in force for eighteen years. The Congregation agreed to do so, and on April 15, 1978, the ban was lifted. It was reversed, the Congregation said, "in view of the many original documents not known in 1959; considering the profoundly changed circumstances, and in view of the opinion of many Polish Ordinaries."

Exactly six months and one day later, Cardinal Wojtyla was elected Pope John Paul II, the first pope from Poland. Father Anthony Mruk, S.J., Postulator of the Cause for Sister Faustina, suggests that it was fortunate that the ban on Divine Mercy devotions had been lifted before Cardinal Wojtyla became pope. As it is, there can be no suggestion of national favoritism in the decision. The cause and apostolate of Sister Faustina Kowalska progressed simply because heaven wanted it so.

On March 28, 1981, another event took place which was crucial to the beatification of Sister Faustina. An American family, the Digans, had arrived in Cracow five days earlier. Maureen and Bob Digan had decided to make a pilgrimage to the tomb and convent of Sister Faustina. They had come with Father Seraphim Michalenko, M.I.C., Vice-Postulator of Sister Faustina's Cause. The Digans wanted to ask for Faustina's intercession with healings.

From the age of fifteen, Maureen had suffered from lymphedema, an incurable and progressive disease which causes severe swelling of the legs. She had undergone fifty operations within ten years, and finally had to have one leg amputated to the hip. Then, the Digans' only child, Bobby, was born with brain damage and had been seriously ill.

On the evening of the twenty-eighth, the Digans and Father Michalenko concluded a novena of prayers, recited the chaplet, and said another prayer for the healing of Maureen and Bobby.

"In my heart," Maureen later reported, "I heard Sister Faustina say, 'Ask for my help and I will help you.'" Suddenly, the pain that Maureen felt constantly was gone. Since she didn't really believe in miracles and had come to Poland primarily to please her husband, she told herself that she must be having a nervous breakdown.

On the following day, she noticed that the swelling in her remaining leg was gone. She stuffed her one shoe with tissues so that no one would notice that it was now too large for her foot. Three or four days later, she finally accepted her healing and a new feeling of intimacy with God.

Back in the United States, the unexplainable and complete reversal of Maureen's disease was verified by five doctors. More than twenty-five friends and relatives of Maureen gave statements about her and her disease to the Archdiocese of Boston. In short, Maureen was healed, and young Bobby had a temporary healing.

"Bobby's vocation in life was different," wrote his mother, Maureen Digan. "He received a dramatic but incomplete healing that allowed him to live an almost normal life for three-and-a-half wonderful years. He was off all medication, learned to ride a bike, and won gold and silver medals in the Special Olympics. Then, his condition worsened and he went to the Lord in May of 1991." Bobby was eighteen years old.

But, as time passed, it was clear that the cure of Maureen Digan was "miraculous." Maureen Digan's healing fit the criteria for a "miraculous cure." A "miraculous cure," according to Father George Kosicki, C.S.B., the Assistant Director of Divine Mercy International, must have three characteristics. It must be: 1) instantaneous; 2) complete and lasting; and 3) attributable to a particular saint. In the Maureen Digan case, the required characteristics of the cure were easily and clearly met. The healing had taken place instantaneously at Sister Faustina's tomb. In time, Maureen Digan's case was submitted to the Congregation for the Causes of the Saints.

On March 7, 1992, Sister Faustina was named a "Venerable" Servant of God by the Congregation in view of her heroic practice of Christian virtues. This was an all-important step on the way to canonization for the Polish nun.

Later in the same year — on December 21 — a decree was published in which the Church announced it was accepting the healing of Maureen Digan as a miracle granted through the intercession of Sister Faustina. At least one miraculous cure attributable to Faustina was needed for her beatification. The Church also announced that "her solemn beatification would take place in Rome on April 18, 1993, the Second Sunday of Easter, which Our Lord had revealed to her as the 'Feast of Mercy.' "

Since Sister Faustina was beatified, the Church has appropriately called her "Blessed Faustina." Now churches can be named after her. Statues or pictures of her may be displayed and Masses may be said in her honor on her feast day, with the permission of the local bishop.

The last segment of Sister Faustina's journey to canonization involves another period of study by the Church. An additional miraculous cure attributable to Blessed Faustina is needed before the Congregation for the Causes of the Saints will authorize the canonization of Blessed Faustina.

In October of 1995, the healing of an American priest, Father Ron Pytel of Baltimore, took place after his parishioners prayed at the tomb of Blessed Faustina in Cracow. Father Pytel, then forty-seven years old, was pastor of Holy Rosary Parish in Baltimore, which houses the Archdiocesan Shrine of Divine Mercy.

Father Pytel had undergone heart surgery in June 1995 to replace an aortic valve that had been almost completely blocked by a calcium build-up. When surgeons replaced the valve with a mechanical "St. Jude valve" at Johns Hopkins Hospital, they found that Father's heart was in very bad shape, despite the surgery.

When a friend, Father Larry Gesy, discussed Father Pytel's recovery with cardiologist Dr. Nicholas Fortuin of Johns Hopkins, the doctor shook his head with regret. "The doctor said that he did not know what kind of life I would be able to resume," Father Pytel recalled, "that I was basically uninsurable. The damage to the left ventricle was very serious, because my heart had been pushed to the maximum before the surgery."

On October 5, 1995, the feast day of Blessed Faustina, Father Pytel attended an evening prayer service. He venerated a relic of Faustina and collapsed, "slain in the spirit." A group of people gathered around him to pray for a healing. A few weeks later, the pastor's astonished doctor told him that his heart was again normal. "I'll see you in a year," the doctor told Father Pytel.

A full canonical inquiry into the case was held by the Archdiocese of Baltimore in 1996. Then the records of the case were taken to the Congregation for the Causes of Saints in Rome by Father Pytel and Father Seraphim Michalenko, M.I.C., the Vice-Postulator. The case is under consideration by the Congregation. But it may not be finally judged as "miraculous" with respect to the precise criteria demanded by the Church. In one percent of patients with Father Pytel's condition who have had surgery, there is a healing of heart muscle over a period of years. For this reason, the Congregation may not see his exceptionally rapid return to health in three months' time as "miraculous."

When the time is right, the Church will likely declare that Blessed Faustina Kowalska is a canonized saint. The young woman whom Jesus called His "Apostle of Divine Mercy" will be universally honored for her faithfulness to Christ. And the message of God's Divine Mercy will become known and familiar all over the world.

16

The Meaning of God's Mercy

"There are truths of the faith which we are supposed to know and which we frequently refer to, but we do not understand them very well, nor do we live by them. It was so with me, concerning the Divine Mercy" — **Father Michael Sopocko.**

Mercy. Although it may have been an elusive truth, the concept of mercy is intimately and profoundly connected with God in the Judeo-Christian tradition.

In Judaism, the ancient Hebrew word *Hesed* has several shades of meaning. It can mean God's faithfulness, His tenderness, His salvation, and His peace. Above all, it means His promise of mercy. But, according to Old Testament scholars, there is another word, *Rachamim* or *rah a mim*, which is used to describe an intimate sort of mercy. It was originally used to describe the boundless and forgiving love of a mother for her child. The Old Testament abounds with examples of God's continuous mercy for the Jews, His Chosen People.

When the Jewish people first encountered God, He was in the process of freeing them from Egyptian slavery. It wasn't that the Jews deserved such treatment. God was acting because He loved them and wanted them to be free. Then God led the Hebrews through the desert and into the Promised Land despite their frequent infidelities. Mercy, the Jews gradually saw, went way beyond what justice would dictate. "Give thanks to the Lord of heaven, for his mercy endures forever," states Psalm 136:26.

In the Old Testament, the Jews were constantly reminded that mercy flows from the very heart of God to His creation. After Jesus came into the world and redeemed a sinful human race, Christian writers and Fathers of the Church soon saw that sending His Son into the world was the crowning, ultimate act of the Creator's mercy. "Your Christ, O God, is Your Mercy," wrote St. Augustine, the fourth-century bishop of Hippo who had converted to Christianity only after years of godless, self-centered living.

"Christ is God's mercy," St. Augustine stated. That Jesus, the Son of God, was much more than a *reflection* of God's mercy took some time to understand. That Jesus *is* mercy, and that God, in all three persons, *is* mercy was not readily assimilated into the mind or heart of Christ's Church. It took centuries for the Church and her theologians and teachers to see the full and glorious truth. And in many respects, the realization that God equals mercy did not truly blossom until modern times. Many theologians, including the spiritual director of Blessed Faustina, have admitted that.

"There are truths of the faith which we are supposed to know and which we frequently refer to, but we do not understand them very well, nor do we live by them," observed Father Michael Sopocko, a professor of theology and the spiritual director of Sister Mary Faustina. "It was so with me, concerning the Divine Mercy."

Father Sopocko, who had earned a doctorate in theology, needed time to consider what he'd been told about mercy's being the preeminent attribute of God. After all, the idea was brought to his attention by a sister who'd had only three semesters of schooling to her credit. At first, the teaching did not seem valid.

"I had not understood and for the moment I could not even agree, that the Divine Mercy is the highest attribute of God, the Creator, Redeemer and Sanctifier," he wrote. But when this priest took the time to study, to search the Scriptures and the writings of the Fathers and Doctors of the Church, he found that what she said was true. Faustina, after all, was tutored by Jesus Christ Himself. It was He who gradually instructed her on the mysteries of His mercy.

Of course, it was vital for Father Sopocko to see and then promote the truth about God's divine mercy. He was the one whom Jesus had pointed out to Sister Faustina. "He will help you to fulfill My will here on earth," Jesus said of Father Sopocko.

It was Father Sopocko who had the Divine Mercy devotions published and distributed. It was he who led Sister Faustina in 1934 to a painter who painted the first Divine Mercy image. And it was Father Sopocko who received the first novices into the Congregation of the Most Merciful Redeemer at Mysilborz after the visionary's death. Later on, the congregation that Sister Faustina had visualized as a contemplative order was modified by the bishop. He wanted a community that was both active and contemplative in nature.

"The Mercy of God is a mystery which reason alone cannot entirely fathom," this same theologian explained in his book *God Is Mercy*, which was published in 1955, many years after the death of Sister Faustina. "Indeed, reason shows us that God is Merciful, but on the other hand, it is unable to penetrate the depths into which Divine Mercy reaches." As hard as we try, God's mercy is beyond our ken — our everyday understanding.

Nonetheless, as Father Sopocko noted, God wants humanity to recognize and really accept His mercy even if it cannot be understood.

"Our Savior did not conceal the Mercy of God, but revealed it through the Incarnation, through His hidden and public life," Father Sopocko wrote. "He emphasized it in His teachings, and above all, He presented it to us vividly through the mystery of the Redemption, by His death on the cross for the sins of the whole world." That mercy, he wrote, is extended to all mankind through the sacraments, sacramentals, indulgences and charisms, gifts, and fruits of the Holy Spirit.

This is why the image or vision which Blessed Faustina called "the image of the Divine Mercy" was an image of Jesus with streams of light flowing out of His chest, the very center of His being. For a while, Sister Faustina herself did not understand the meaning of those beautiful red and white rays of light. Jesus told her.

"The two rays denote Blood and Water. The pale ray stands for the Water which makes souls righteous. The red ray stands for the Blood which is the life of souls. These two rays issued forth from the depths of My tender mercy when My agonized Heart was opened by a lance on the Cross." When He spoke of the Water and the Blood, Jesus was referring to the sacraments, especially baptism, the Eucharist, and reconciliation.

In the *Catechism of the Catholic Church*, the idea that sacraments flow out from the very heart of the Redeemer is confirmed. "The Church affirms that for believers the sacraments of the New Covenant are *necessary for salvation*. 'Sacramental grace' is the grace of the Holy Spirit, given by Christ and proper to each sacrament. The fruit of sacramental life is that the Spirit of adoption makes the faithful partakers in the divine nature by uniting them in a living union with the only Son, the Savior" (CCC 1129).

Those rays, symbolizing the sacraments, unite us "in a living union with the only Son, the Savior," the Church tells us. Those rays are the life of Christ, and Christ, the Son of God, is Mercy.

Truthfully, however, it wasn't as though Christians and other people had no understanding or familiarity at all with mercy. Mercy was — and is — seen as charitable action towards another.

"We call a man merciful when he shows compassion for his neighbor and does all he can to lighten his burdens whether material or spiritual.

Mercy, as compassion, is even manifested in animals. For instance, a dog will whimper at the sight of its sick master," explained Father Sopocko. But, "God's mercy is neither compassion or virtue."

As a pure spirit, God isn't subject to emotions or affections. God is self-sufficient and perfectly happy. And God can't grow in virtue because He is already all-good. "Divine mercy is God's perfection or attribute in which He willingly inclines Himself toward His creatures to ward off impending miseries and to satisfy their daily need."

John Paul II spoke to youth at St. Ann's Church in Warsaw on June 3, 1979, during his first pilgrimage to Poland. The Divine Mercy is displayed behind him.

Pope John Paul II, more than any other pontiff in modern times, saw that the world needed to see and embrace God Who is mercy. In fact, he has seen it as the guiding command of his pontificate to articulate and explain this truth. Father George Kosicki, C.S.B., assistant director for the Divine Mercy International Apostolate at Eden Hill, Stockbridge, Massachusetts, called Pope John Paul "the Mercy Pope." But John Paul has essentially given himself that title.

On November 22, 1981, at the Shrine of Merciful Love near Todi, Italy, the pope said, "Right from the beginning of my ministry in St. Peter's See in Rome I considered this message (the mercy of God) my special task. Providence has assigned it to me in the present situation of man, the Church and the world." This pope's reign had begun on October 16, 1978.

Why did this Holy Father so emphatically connect his pontificate with the mercy of God? Six months earlier, on May 13, in St. Peter's Square, the pope had come close to death. An assassination attempt severely wounded him, putting a bullet into his abdomen. The would-be assassin, Mehmet Ali Agha, could not believe that the pope had survived. He had shot to kill. John Paul II credited his survival to the mercy of God and the special intervention of Our Lady of Fatima. He had been shot on the Feast of Our Lady of Fatima.

During his recuperation, the pope had the documents on Fatima brought to him. Later still, he asked for the diary of Sister Faustina and had it read to him in Polish. The pope understood that Mary's appearances at Fatima in 1917 took place to warn the world to repent. Men and women had to be reminded to throw themselves upon the mercy of God and reform their lives. But Blessed Faustina's long and beautiful diary echoed the Fatima messages. John Paul may not have read the diary before. Now, as he was recuperating in a hospital in Rome, it struck him with great force.

Faustina's diary urged the world to embrace penance and sufferings. Believers were to pray for one another — most especially for the dying and for the souls in purgatory. Prayer and a return to the sacraments would open the floodgates of mercy for mankind. God wanted mercy to rain down upon the earth.

Even before the attempt on his life, however, the pope was committed to reminding the world about God's mercy. As a seminarian, priest, and bishop, he had often visited the grave of Sister Faustina, the "Apostle of Divine Mercy." Recognition of God's mercy for His creation became a part of him, and he gradually realized that it was a truth that needed great emphasis in our times. The pontiff's second encyclical, *Dives in Misericordia* ("Rich in Mercy"), appeared only two years after his election to Peter's chair.

In the first sentence of this letter, the pope proclaimed that " 'God rich in mercy' is the God whom Jesus Christ revealed to us as Father. Moreover, it was in himself, the Son, that Jesus shows us this God and made Him known to us."

Like the spiritual director of Sister Faustina, the pope said that Jesus is the primary manifestation of God's mercy. When the Lord was asked by the disciples of John the Baptist if He was the Messiah, Jesus answered indirectly. He told John's followers to tell John about His deeds — His works of mercy. "The blind recover their sight, cripples walk, lepers are cured, the deaf hear, dead men are raised to life, and the poor have the good news preached to them" (Luke 7:22-23).

Jesus is the reflection of God, and God is mercy. But Jesus also taught that the children of God should reflect — or be images — of Mercy.

This demand to be merciful, wrote Pope John Paul, "is an essential element in the messianic message and the heart of the gospel ethos. The Master enunciates this requirement in the form of a commandment which He describes as 'the greatest and first' but also in the form of a blessing, when He says in the Sermon on the Mount: 'Blest are they who show mercy; mercy shall be theirs' (Matthew 5:7)."

In a special way, the pope explained, a lesson about the mercy of God shines forth in the parable of the Prodigal Son in the Gospel of Luke. In this parable, Pope John Paul II said, "the innermost nature of divine mercy emerges with special clarity even though the word 'mercy' does not occur." The boundless love of the father for his son brings new life. A return to life. That is the way the father explains his actions to his angry older son. "We had to celebrate and rejoice! This brother of yours was dead and has come back to life. He was lost and is found" (Matthew 15:32).

That God's mercy could bring new life to a world dying, steeped in its own evils, was something that Blessed Faustina Kowalska gradually learned. She had many visions depicting the evil state of the world. In her own body, in a very literal way, she experienced pains when she was near a person who had fallen from grace.

Jesus wanted her to become more and more like Him. He often appeared to her with His crown of thorns and with open wounds. She understood that she, too, was to suffer greatly in reparation for sinners. "I want your last moments to be completely similar to mine on the cross," Jesus told her. "There is but one price at which souls are bought and that is suffering united to my suffering on the cross."

Faustina suffered and prayed to change the hearts of sinners so that they could receive God's mercy. There was a never-ending supply of mercy in God, but there was justice, too, because justice was also an attribute of

God. When Jesus returns at the end of time as a Judge, the time for Mercy will have expired.

And of all the traits of God, mercy is His supreme attribute.

St. Thomas Aquinas, whom Sister Faustina surely had never studied, taught that the Mercy of God is the chief motive for God's exterior actions. And mercy is behind every work of the Creator. "Since God has no superior and no one to whom He could subordinate Himself through love, therefore His highest perfection is not Love, but Mercy," wrote Father Sopocko, summarizing the teachings of the Angelic Doctor.

The truth about mercy which St. Thomas Aquinas presented in brilliant philosophical arguments more than seven hundred years ago is the same truth which an uneducated Polish sister quietly proclaimed through her sufferings and diary. God is love, and love, put into action, is mercy.

On the day of Sister Faustina's beatification, April 18, 1993, Pope John Paul II declared that the simple sister's witness on behalf of Divine Mercy couldn't be more timely.

"It is truly marvelous how her devotion to the merciful Jesus is spreading in our contemporary world and gaining so many human hearts," the pope said. "This is doubtlessly a sign of the times — a sign of our twentieth century. The balance of this century which is now ending, in addition to the advances which have often surpassed those of preceding eras, presents a deep restlessness and fear of the future. Where, if not in The Divine Mercy, can the world find refuge and the light of hope?"

17

The Words of
Sister Faustina

Compassion for the Sick

In a suffering soul, we should see Jesus Crucified, and not a loafer or burden on the community. A soul who suffers with submission to the will of God draws down more blessing on the whole convent than all the working sisters.

What the Angels Envy

If the angels were capable of envy, they would envy us for two things: one is receiving of Holy Communion, and the other is suffering.

Strength in Weakness

When one is ill and weak, one must constantly make efforts to measure up to what others are doing as a matter of course. But even those matter-of-course things cannot always be managed. Nevertheless, thank You, Jesus, for everything, because it is not the greatness of the works, but the greatness of the effort that will be rewarded. What is done out of love is not small.

Charity Given to the Poor

Something more is given when giving nothing, than when giving much in a rude manner.

Importance of Obedience

The disobedient soul exposes itself to great misfortunes; it will make no progress toward perfection, nor will it succeed in the spiritual life. God lavishes His graces most generously on the soul, but it must be an obedient soul.

Silence in Religious Life

The tongue is a small member, but it does big things. A religious who does not keep silence will never attain holiness; that is she will never become a saint. . . . But in order to hear the voice of God, one has to have silence in one's soul and to keep silence; not a gloomy silence, but an interior silence; that is to say, recollection in God. One can speak a great deal without breaking silence and, on the contrary, one can speak little and be constantly breaking silence. Oh, what irreparable damage is done by the breach of silence! We cause a lot of harm to our neighbor, but even more to our own selves.

Prayer for the Dying

Although it give us eternal life, death is dreadful . . . Oh, if only everyone realized how great the Lord's mercy is and how much we all need that mercy, especially at that crucial hour. . . . In a strange way, the Lord Jesus makes known to me that a dying soul has need of my prayer. I feel vividly and clearly that spirit who is asking me for prayer. I was not aware that souls are so closely united, and often it is my Guardian Angel who tells me.

A Daily Eucharist

Every morning during meditation, I prepare myself for the whole day's struggle. Holy Communion assures me that I will win the victory; and so it is. I fear the day when I do not receive Holy Communion. This Bread of the Strong gives me all the strength I need to carry on my mission and the courage to do whatever the Lord asks of me. The courage and strength that are in me are not of me, but of Him who lives in me — it is the Eucharist.

Christ's Special Love for Poland

As I was praying for Poland, I heard these words: "I bear a special love for Poland, and if she will be obedient to My will, I will exalt her in might and holiness. From her will come forth a spark that will prepare the world for My final coming."

Love of God

God has given me to understand that there is but one thing that is of infinite value in His eyes, and that is love of God; love, love and once again, love; and nothing can compare with a single act of pure love of God.

Confessing Little Faults

There is nothing little in the spiritual life. Sometimes a seemingly insignificant thing will disclose a matter of great consequence and will be for the confessor a beam of light which helps him to get to know the soul. Many spiritual undertones are concealed in little things.

Priests

The Lord Jesus greatly protects His representatives on earth. How closely He is united with them; and He orders me to give priority to their opinion over His. I have come to know the great intimacy which exists between Jesus and His priests. Jesus defends whatever the priest says, and often complies with his wishes, and sometimes makes His own relationship with a soul depend on the priest's advice. O Jesus, through a special grace, I have come to know very clearly to what extent You have shared Your power and mystery with them, more so than with the Angels. I rejoice in this, for it is all for my good.

When Troubles Come

In the midst of the worst difficulties and adversities, I do not lose inner peace or exterior balance, and this discourages my adversaries. Patience in adversity gives power to the soul.

The Mercy of Christ

(words of Jesus given to Sister Faustina)

My mercy is greater than your sins and those of the entire world. Who can measure the extent of My goodness? For you, I descended from heaven to earth; for you I allowed Myself to be nailed to the cross; for you I let My Sacred Heart be pierced with a lance, thus opening wide the source of mercy for you. Come, then, with trust to draw graces from this fountain. I never reject a contrite heart. Your misery has disappeared in the depths of My mercy. Do not argue with Me about your wretchedness. You will give Me pleasure if you hand over to Me all your troubles and griefs. I shall heap upon you the treasures of My grace.

A Tragic Worldliness

My Jesus, how little these people talk about You. They talk about every-thing but You, Jesus. And if they talk so little [about You], it is quite prob-able that they do not think about You at all. The whole world interests them; but about You, their Creator, there is silence.

The Power of Example

I strive for the greatest perfection possible in order to be useful to the Church. Greater by far is my bond to the Church. The sanctity or the fall of each individual soul has an effect upon the whole Church. Observing myself and those who are close to me, I have come to understand how great an influence I have on other souls, not by any heroic deeds, as these are striking in themselves, but by small actions like the movement of the hand, a look, and many other things too numerous to mention, which have an effect on and reflect in the souls of others, as I myself have noticed.

Battling against Satan

I want no respite in this battle, but I shall fight to the last breath for the glory of my King and Lord. I shall not lay the sword aside until He calls me before His throne; I fear no blows, because God is my shield. It is the enemy who should fear us, and not we him. Satan defeats only the proud and the cowardly, because the humble are strong. Nothing will confuse or frighten a humble soul. I have directed my flight at the very center of the sun's heat, and nothing can lower its course. Love will not allow itself to be taken prisoner; it is free like a queen. Love attains God.

Humility, a Precious Virtue

Lord, although You often make know to me the thunders of Your anger, Your anger vanishes before lowly souls. Although You are great, Lord, You allow Yourself to be overcome by a lowly and deeply humble soul. O humility, the most precious of virtues, how few souls possess you! I see only a semblance of this virtue everywhere, but not the virtue itself. Lord, reduce me to nothingness in my own eyes that I may find grace in Yours.

Sacrament of Reconciliation

(words of Jesus to Faustina)

When you go to confession, to this fountain of My mercy, the Blood and Water which came forth from My Heart always flows down upon your soul and ennobles it. Every time you go to confession, immerse yourself entirely in My mercy, with great trust, so that I may pour the bounty of My grace upon your soul. When you approach the confessional, know this, that I Myself am waiting there for you. I am only hidden in the priest, but I Myself act in your soul. Here the misery of the soul meets the God of mercy.

(From *Diary, Divine Mercy in My Soul*)

18

Prayers of
Blessed Faustina

The titles for these prayers have been written by the author — CMO.

A Prayer for Merciful Hands and Feet

Help me, O Lord, that my hands may be merciful and filled with good deeds, so that I may do only good to my neighbors and take upon myself the more difficult and toilsome tasks.

Help me, that my feet may be merciful, so that I may hurry to assist my neighbor, overcoming my own fatigue and weariness. My true rest is in the service of my neighbor.

Composed during her last illness in January 1937

To God, I Give the Present Moment

When I look into the future, I am frightened,
But why plunge into the future?
Only the present moment is precious to me,
As the future may never enter my soul at all.
It is no longer in my power,
To change, correct or add to the past;
For neither sages nor prophets could do that.
And so, what the past has embraced I must entrust to God.
O present moment, you belong to me, whole and entire.
I desire to use you as best I can.
And although I am weak and small,
You (God) grant me the grace of your omnipotence.
And so, trusting in Your mercy,
I walk through life like a little child,
Offering You each day this heart
Burning with love for Your greater glory.

July 1931

Prayer for My Native Land

Most merciful Jesus, I beseech You through the intercession of Your Saints, and especially the intercession of Your dearest Mother who nurtured You from childhood, bless my native land. I beg You, Jesus, look not on our sins, but on the tears of little children, on the hunger and cold they suffer. Jesus, for the sake of these little ones, grant me the grace that I am asking of You for my country.

1934

In Praise of God's Mercy

Praise the Lord, my soul, for everything, and glorify His mercy, for His goodness is without end. Everything will pass, but His mercy is without limit or end. And although evil will attain its measure, in mercy there is no measure.

O my God, even in the punishments You send down upon the earth I see the abyss of Your mercy, for by punishing us here on earth You free us from eternal punishment. Rejoice, all you creatures, for you are closer to God in His infinite mercy than a baby to its mother's heart. O God, you are compassion itself for the greatest sinners who sincerely repent. The greater the sinner, the greater his right to God's mercy.

April 28, 1935

My Longing Soul

With longing I gaze into the starlit sky,
Into the sapphire of fathomless firmaments.
There the pure heart leaps out to find You, O God,
And yearns to be freed of the bonds of the flesh.

With great longing, I gaze upon you, my homeland.
When will this, my exile, come to an end?
O Jesus, such is the call of Your bride
Who suffers agony in her thirst for You.

With longing, I gaze at the footprints of the saints
Who crossed this wilderness on their way to the fatherland.
They left me the example of their virtue and their counsels,
And they say to me, "Patience, Sister, soon the fetters will break."

But my longing soul hears not these words.
Ardently; it yearns for its Lord and its God,
And it understands not human language,
Because it is enamored of Him alone.

My longing soul, wounded with love,
Forces its way through all created things
And unites itself with infinite eternity,
With the Lord whom my heart has espoused.

Allow my longing soul, O God,
To be drowned in Your Divine Three-fold Essence.
Fulfill my desires, for which I humbly beg You,
With a heart brimming with love's fire.

September 1937

You Are My Helmsman, O God

The barque of my life sails along
Amid darkness and shadows of night,
And I see no shore;
I am sailing the high seas.

The slightest storm would drown me,
Engulfing my boat in the swirling depths,
If You yourself did not watch over me, O God,
at each instant and moment of my life.

Amid the roaring waves
I sail peacefully, trustingly,
And gaze like a child into the distance without fear,
Because You, O Jesus, are my Light.

Dread and terror is all about me,
But within my soul is peace more profound that the depths of the sea,
For he who is with You, O Lord, will not perish;
Of this Your love assures me, O God.
Though a host of dangers surround me,
None of them do I fear, for I fix my gaze on the starry sky,
And I sail along bravely and merrily,
As becomes a pure heart.

And if the ship of my life sails so peacefully,
This is due to but one thing above all:
You are my helmsman, O God.
This I confess with utmost humility.

October 1937

I Am a Host in Your Hand

I am a host in Your hand,
O Jesus, my Creator and Lord,
Silent, hidden, without beauty or charm,
Because all the beauty of my soul is imprinted within me.

I am a host in Your hand, O Divine Priest,
Do with me as You please;
I am totally dependent on Your will, O Lord
Because it is the delight and adornment of my soul.

I am like a white host in Your hand, O God,
I implore You, transform me into Yourself.
May I be wholly hidden in You,
Locked in Your merciful Heart as in Heaven.

I am like a host in Your hand, O Eternal Priest,
May the wafer of my body hide me from human eye;
May Your eye alone measure my love and devotion,
Because my heart is always united with Your Divine Heart.
I am like a sacrificial host in Your hand, O Divine Mediator,
And I burn on the altar of holocaust,
Crushed and ground by suffering like grains of wheat,
And all this for the sake of Your glory, for the salvation of souls.

I am a host abiding in the tabernacle of Your Heart.
I go through life drowned in Your love,
And I fear nothing in the world,
For You Yourself are my shield, my strength and my defense.

I am a host, laid on the altar of Your Heart,
To burn forever with the fire of love,
For I know that You have lifted me up solely because of Your mercy,
And so I turn all these gifts and graces to Your glory.

I am a host in Your hand, O Judge and Savior.
In the last hour of my life,
May the omnipotence of Your grace lead me to my goal,
May Your compassion on the vessel of mercy become famous.

Spring 1938

Through Mary, a Pure Crystal

Unfathomable and incomprehensible in Your mercy,
For love of us You take on flesh
From the Immaculate Virgin, ever untouched by sin,
Because You have willed it so from all ages.

The Blessed Virgin, that Snow-White Lily,
Is first to praise the omnipotence of Your mercy.
Her pure heart opens with love for the coming of the Word;
She believes the words of God's messenger and is confirmed in trust.

Heaven is astounded that God has become man,
That there is on earth a heart worthy of God Himself.
Why is it that You do not unite Yourself with a Seraph, but with a sinner,
    O Lord ?
Oh, because, despite the purity of the virginal womb,
this is a mystery of Your mercy.

O mystery of God's mercy, O God of compassion,
That You have deigned to leave the heavenly throne
And to stoop down to our misery, to human weakness,
For it is not the angels, but man who needs mercy.

To give worthy praise to the Lord's mercy,
We unite ourselves with Your Immaculate Mother,
For then our hymn will be more pleasing to You,
Because She is chosen from among men and angels.

Through Her, as through a pure crystal,
Your mercy was passed on to us.
Through Her, man became pleasing to God;
Through Her, streams of grace flowed down upon us.

1938

19

The Divine Mercy Message and Devotion: Chaplet, Novena, and Mercy Sunday

Our Lord taught Blessed Faustina special ways to live out the response to His mercy. These we call the devotion to The Divine Mercy. The word "devotion" means fulfilling our vows. It is a commitment of our lives to the Lord, who is Mercy itself. By giving our lives to The Divine Mercy — Jesus Christ Himself — we become instruments of His mercy to others, and so we can live out the command of the Lord: "Be merciful even as your Father is merciful" (Luke 6:36).

Devotions are to lead to devotion. Devotions are prayers and various gestures and practices that are intended to help us to a fuller commitment to the Lord. So the image of the merciful Savior is to remind us of the demands of the Lord to be merciful and trust in Him. The devotional prayers and objects are not ends in themselves, but are ways of growing in love of the Lord.

The Divine Mercy Chaplet

Blessed Faustina prayed the Divine Mercy Chaplet almost constantly, especially for the dying. The Lord urged her to encourage others to say it too, promising extraordinary graces to those who would recite this special prayer.

The essential prayers of the Chaplet were given to Sister Faustina during a vision she experienced on the evening of September 13, 1935. As Sister Faustina reported in her diary (474-476), an angel appeared, and she understood immediately that his mission from God was to punish sinners on earth.

The words of an intercessory prayer came to Faustina's mind and heart, and she began to pray it. Then, she saw that the angel's striking arm was held back. "Never before had I prayed with such inner power as I did then," she said.

The Chaplet of Mercy is recited using ordinary rosary beads of five decades.

Opening Prayers (Optional)

You expired, Jesus, but the source of life gushed forth for souls, and the ocean of mercy opened up for the whole world. O Fount of Life, unfathomable Divine Mercy, envelop the whole world and empty Yourself out upon us.

Diary, 1319, given to Sister Faustina in 1937

O Blood and Water, which gushed forth from the Heart of Jesus as a fountain of mercy for us, I trust in You!

Diary, 84, given to Sister Faustina in 1934

On the three beads near the cross of the rosary, say: the Our Father, the Hail Mary, and the Apostles' Creed. These prayers express our dependence on our loving Father, an appeal to Mary, the sinless Mother of God, for her merciful intercession at the hour of our death, and finally, our faith in the dogmas of the Church.

The Our Father

Our Father, who art in heaven, hallowed be thy name. Thy kingdom come; thy will be done on earth as it is in heaven. Give us this day our daily bread; and forgive us our trespasses as we forgive those who trespass against us; and lead us not into temptation, but deliver us from evil. Amen.

The Hail Mary

Hail Mary, full of grace, the Lord is with thee; blessed art thou among women, and blessed is the fruit of thy womb, Jesus. Holy Mary, Mother of God, pray for us sinners, now and at the hour of our death. Amen.

The Apostles' Creed

I believe in God, the Father almighty, creator of heaven and earth.

I believe in Jesus Christ, his only Son, our Lord.

He was conceived by the power of the Holy Spirit and was born of the
Virgin Mary.

He suffered under Pontius Pilate, was crucified, died, and was buried.
He descended to the dead.
On the third day he rose again.
He ascended into heaven, and is seated at the right hand of the Father.
He will come again to judge the living and the dead.
I believe in the Holy Spirit, the holy Catholic Church, the communion
of saints, the forgiveness of sins, the resurrection of the body, and the
life everlasting. Amen.

On the large bead before each "decade," or group of ten beads, say:
Eternal Father, I offer You the Body and Blood, Soul and Divinity of
Your dearly beloved Son, Our Lord Jesus Christ, in atonement for our sins
and those of the whole world.

Diary, 475, given to Sister Faustina in September 1935

Then, on each of the ten small beads of each decade, recite:
For the sake of His sorrowful Passion, have mercy on us and on the
whole world.

Diary, 476, given to Sister Faustina in September 1935

At the end of the chaplet, pray the following prayer three times:
Holy God, Holy Mighty One, Holy Immortal One, have mercy on us
and on the whole world.

Diary, 475, given to Sister Faustina in September 1935

Closing Prayer (Optional)

Eternal God, in whom mercy is endless and the treasury of compassion
inexhaustible, look kindly upon us and increase Your mercy in us, that in
difficult moments we might not despair nor become despondent, but with
great confidence submit ourselves to Your holy will, which is Love and
Mercy itself.

Diary, 950, given to Sister Faustina in 1937

Sister Faustina was told to share the Chaplet prayer with others. "Encourage souls to say the Chaplet which I have given you," Jesus told her.
"Whoever will recite it will receive great mercy at the hour of death. When
they say this chaplet in the presence of the dying, I will stand between My
Father and the dying person, not as the just Judge but as the Merciful Savior. I desire to grant unimaginable graces to those souls who trust in My
mercy."

"Prayed on ordinary rosary beads, the Chaplet of Divine Mercy is an intercessory prayer that extends the offering of the Eucharist, so it is especially appropriate to use it after having received Holy Communion," suggested Father Seraphim Michalenko, M.I.C., and Vinny Flynn in *The Divine Mercy Message and Devotion*, a booklet about the Divine Mercy devotions.

The Hour of Great Mercy — 3:00 p.m.

The visionary also later learned that it was especially beneficial to pray the Chaplet at 3:00 p.m., the hour at which Jesus died on the cross. In her diary, Sister wrote that Jesus had explained it this way. "At three o'clock, implore My mercy, especially for sinners; and if only for a brief moment, immerse yourself in My Passion, particularly in My abandonment at the moment of agony. This is the hour of great mercy for the whole world. In this hour, I will refuse nothing to the soul that makes a request of Me in virtue of My passion" (*Diary*, 1320).

Prayer at 3:00 p.m., or during the 3:00 to 4:00 p.m. "Hour of Great Mercy" is becoming an increasingly popular devotion. Many people pray the chaplet at 3:00 p.m. Others pray other prayers or simply meditate for a while on the sacrifice and death of Jesus on the cross. In the Philippines, for instance, this custom has become relatively widespread in recent years.

Still another way in which Faustina began to use the chaplet was in a novena.

The Novena to the Divine Mercy

Our Lord told her to pray the chaplet each day for nine days as a Novena to the Divine Mercy. He told her that He particularly wanted the Mercy Novena prayed on the nine days before Mercy Sunday, the Sunday after Easter. Those who say the novena at this time should begin the novena on Good Friday and say it each day through the Saturday before Mercy Sunday.

On Good Friday, 1937, Jesus dictated nine special intentions He wished to add to chaplets in the novena said for Mercy Sunday (*Diary*, 1209-1229). "On each day you will bring to my Heart a different group of souls, and you will immerse them in this ocean of My mercy, and I will bring all these souls into the house of My Father," Jesus promised.

Novena Intentions and Prayers

First Day Intention: All Mankind

"Today, bring to Me *all mankind, especially all sinners* and immerse them in the ocean of My mercy. In this way you will console Me in the bitter grief into which the loss of souls plunges Me."

First Day Prayer: "Most merciful Jesus, whose very nature it is to have compassion on us and to forgive us, do not look upon our sins but upon our trust which we place in Your infinite goodness. Receive us all into the abode of Your Most Compassionate Heart, and never let us escape from it. We beg this of You by Your love which unites You to the Father and the Holy Spirit.

Eternal Father, turn Your merciful gaze upon all mankind and especially upon poor sinners, all enfolded in the Most Compassionate Heart of Jesus. For the sake of His sorrowful Passion show us Your mercy, that we may praise the omnipotence of Your mercy for ever and ever. Amen.

Second Day Intention: Priests and Religious
"Today, bring to Me *the Souls of priests and religious* and immerse them in My unfathomable mercy. It was they who gave Me strength to endure My bitter Passion. Through them, as through channels, My mercy flows out upon mankind."

Second Day Prayer: Most Merciful Jesus, from whom comes all that is good, increase Your grace in men and women consecrated to Your service, that they may perform worthy works of mercy; and that all who see them may glorify the Father of Mercy who is in heaven.

Eternal Father, turn Your merciful gaze upon the company of chosen ones in Your vineyard — upon the souls of priests and religious; and endow them with the strength of Your blessing. For the love of the Heart of Your son in which they are enfolded, impart to them Your power and light, that they may be able to guide others in the way of salvation and with one voice sing praise to Your boundless mercy for ages without end. Amen.

Third Day Intention: Devout and Faithful Souls
"Today, bring to Me *all devout and faithful souls* and immerse them in the ocean of My mercy. These souls brought Me consolation on the Way of the Cross. They were the drop of consolation in the midst of an ocean of bitterness."

Third Day Prayer: Most Merciful Jesus, from the treasury of Your mercy, You impart Your graces in great abundance to each and all. Receive us into the abode of Your Most Compassionate Heart and never let us escape from It. We beg this grace of You by the most wondrous love for the heavenly Father with which Your Heart burns so fiercely.

Eternal Father, turn Your merciful gaze upon faithful souls, as upon the inheritance of Your Son. For the sake of His sorrowful Passion, grant them Your blessing and surround them with Your constant protection. Thus may they never fail in love or lose the treasure of the holy faith, but rather, with all the hosts of Angels and Saints, may they glorify Your boundless mercy for endless ages. Amen.

Fourth Day Intention: Unbelievers

"Today bring to Me *those who do not believe in God and those who do not yet know Me.* I was thinking also of them during My bitter Passion, and their future zeal comforted My Heart. Immerse them in the ocean of My mercy."

Fourth Day Prayer: Most compassionate Jesus, You are the Light of the whole world. Receive into the abode of Your Most Compassionate Heart the souls of those who do not believe in God and of those who as yet do not know You. Let the rays of Your grace enlighten them that they, too, together with us, may extol Your wonderful mercy; and do not let them escape from the abode which is Your Most Compassionate Heart.

Eternal Father, turn Your merciful gaze upon the souls of those who do not believe in You, and of those who as yet do not know You, but who are enclosed in the Most Compassionate Heart of Jesus. Draw them to the light of the Gospel. These souls do not know what great happiness it is to love You. Grant that they, too, may extol the generosity of Your mercy for endless ages. Amen.

Fifth Day Intention: Those Who Do Not Practice Their Faith

"Today, bring to Me *the souls of those who have separated themselves from My Church* and immerse them in the ocean of My mercy. During My bitter Passion they tore at My Body and Heart, that is My Church. As they return to unity with the Church, My wounds heal and in this way they alleviate My Passion."

Fifth Day Prayer: Most Merciful Jesus, Goodness Itself, You do not refuse light to those who seek it of You. Receive into the abode of Your Most Compassionate Heart the souls of those who have separated themselves from Your Church. Draw them by Your light into the unity of the Church and do not let them escape from the abode of Your Most Compassionate Heart; but bring it about that they, too, will come to glorify the generosity of Your mercy.

Eternal Father, turn Your merciful gaze upon the souls of those who have separated themselves from Your Son's Church, who have squandered Your blessings and misused Your graces by obstinately persisting in their errors. Do not look upon their errors, but upon the love of Your own Son and upon His bitter Passion, which He underwent for their sake, since they, too, are enclosed in His Most Compassionate Heart. Bring it about that they also may glorify Your great mercy for endless ages. Amen.

Sixth Day Intention: Children and the Meek

"Today, bring to Me *the meek and humble souls and the souls of little children,* and immerse them in My mercy. These souls most closely resemble My Heart. They strengthened Me during My bitter agony. I saw them as earthly Angels, who will keep vigil at My altars. I pour out upon them whole torrents of grace. Only the humble soul is capable of receiving My grace. I favor humble souls with My confidence."

Sixth Day Prayer: Most Merciful Jesus, You yourself have said, "Learn from Me for I am meek and humble of heart." Receive into the abode of Your Most Compassionate Heart all the meek and humble souls and all the souls of little children. These souls send all heaven into ecstasy and they are the heavenly Father's favorites. They are a sweet-smelling bouquet before the throne of God; God Himself takes delight in their fragrance. These souls have a permanent abode in Your Most Compassionate Heart, O Jesus, and they unceasingly sing out a hymn of love and mercy.

Eternal Father, turn Your merciful gaze upon meek souls, upon humble souls, and upon little children who are enfolded in the abode which is the Most Compassionate Heart of Jesus. These souls bear the closest resemblance to Your Son. Their fragrance rises from the earth and reaches Your very throne. Father of mercy and of all goodness, I beg You by the love You bear these souls and by the delight You take in them: Bless the whole world, that all souls together may sing out the praises of Your mercy for endless ages. Amen.

Seventh Day Intention: Lovers of Mercy

"Today, bring to Me *the souls who especially venerate and glorify My mercy,* and immerse them in My mercy. These souls sorrowed most over my Passion and entered most deeply into My spirit. They are living images of My Compassionate Heart. These souls will shine with a special brightness in the next life. Not one of them will go into the fire of hell. I shall particularly defend each one of them at the hour of death."

Seventh Day Prayer: Most Merciful Jesus, whose Heart is Love Itself, receive into the abode of Your Most Compassionate Heart the souls of those who particularly extol and venerate the greatness of Your mercy. These souls are mighty with the very power of God Himself. In the midst of all afflictions and adversities they go forward, confident of Your mercy; and united to You, O Jesus, they carry all mankind on their shoulders. These souls will not be judged severely, but Your mercy will embrace them as they depart from this life.

Eternal Father, turn Your merciful gaze upon the souls who glorify and venerate Your greatest attribute, that of Your fathomless mercy, and who are enclosed in the Most Compassionate Heart of Jesus. These souls are a living Gospel; their hands are full of deeds of mercy, and their hearts, overflowing with joy, sing a canticle of mercy to You, O Most High! I beg You, O God: Show them Your mercy according to the hope and trust they have placed in You. Let there be accomplished in them the promise of Jesus, Who said to them that during their life, but especially at the hour of death, the souls who will venerate this fathomless mercy of His, He Himself will defend as His glory. Amen.

Eighth Day Intention: Souls in Purgatory

"Today bring to Me *the souls who are detained in Purgatory,* and immerse them in the abyss of My mercy. Let the torrents of My Blood cool down their scorching flames. All these souls are greatly loved by Me. They are making retribution to My justice. It is in your power to bring them relief. Draw all indulgences from the treasury of the Church and offer them on their behalf. Oh, if you only knew the torments they suffer, you would continually offer for them the alms of the spirit and pay off their debt to My justice."

Eighth Day Prayer: Most Merciful Jesus, You Yourself have said that You desire mercy; so I bring into the abode of Your Most Compassionate Heart the souls in Purgatory, souls who are very dear to You, and yet, who must make retribution to Your justice. May the streams of Blood and Water which gushed forth from Your Heart put out the flames of Purgatory, that there, too, the power of Your mercy may be celebrated.

Eternal Father, turn Your merciful gaze upon the souls suffering in Purgatory, who are enfolded in the Most Compassionate Heart of Jesus. I beg You, by the sorrowful Passion of Jesus Your Son, and by all the bitterness with which His most sacred Soul was flooded: Manifest your mercy to the souls who are under Your just scrutiny. Look upon them in no other way but only through the Wounds of Jesus, Your dearly beloved Son; for we firmly believe that there is no limit to Your goodness and compassion. Amen.

Ninth Day Intention: The Lukewarm

"Today, bring to Me *souls who have become lukewarm,* and immerse them in the abyss of My mercy. These souls wound My Heart most painfully. My soul suffered the most dreadful loathing in the Garden of Olives because of lukewarm souls. They were the reason I cried out: 'Father, take this cup away from Me, if it be Your will.' For them the last hope of salvation is to run to My mercy."

Ninth Day Prayer: Most compassionate Jesus, You are Compassion Itself. I bring lukewarm souls into the abode of Your Most Compassionate Heart. In this fire of Your pure love, let these tepid souls, who, like corpses, filled You with such deep loathing, be once again set aflame. O Most Compassionate Jesus, exercise the omnipotence of Your mercy and draw them into the very ardor of Your love, and bestow upon them the gift of holy love, for nothing is beyond Your power.

Eternal Father, turn Your merciful gaze upon lukewarm souls who are nonetheless enfolded in the Most Compassionate Heart of Jesus. Father of Mercy, I beg You by the bitter Passion of Your Son and by His three-hour agony on the Cross: Let them, too, glorify the abyss of Your mercy. Amen.

The Divine Feast of Mercy
(Mercy Sunday)

On fourteen different occasions, according to the diary of Sister Faustina, Jesus asked for the celebration of a "Feast of Mercy." She first became aware that Jesus wanted this feast when she received the vision of Jesus as the Divine Mercy image on February 22, 1931.

That Divine Mercy Image of Jesus was painted in 1934 by Eugene Kazimierowski, a friend of Father Michael Sopocko who was Sister Faustina's spiritual director and confessor. The image was publicly displayed for the first time during a Feast of Mercy in Vilnius. The Feast fell on April 28, 1935, and was celebrated at the church at Ostra Brama, the Eastern (or Dawn) Gate. Sister Faustina accompanied her fellow sisters to a three-day celebration, marking the end of the Jubilee Year of Redemption and Divine Mercy Sunday. On Divine Mercy Sunday, Father Sopocko preached a homily on God's great mercy.

But the Lord apparently wanted Mercy Sunday celebrated each year in each church. It was to be done in the following way:

1. Veneration of an image of Jesus, The Divine Mercy. "I want the image to be solemnly blessed on the first Sunday after Easter, and I want it to be venerated publicly so that every soul may know about it," Jesus told His "Apostle of Divine Mercy" (*Diary*, 341). Veneration has historically meant a gesture of respect such as a bow or a genuflection on the knee or knees.

2. Celebration at a Feast of Mercy Mass and the reception of Holy Communion.

3. Celebration of the Sacrament of Reconciliation, preferably before Mercy Sunday.

4. Extending mercy to others through words, actions, and prayers following the Feast of Mercy.

Heaven apparently wanted the world to know that the mercy of God flows unceasingly through the sacraments of Eucharist and Reconciliation. Jesus advised Sister Faustina that: "I want to grant a complete pardon to the souls that will go to Confession and receive Holy Communion on the Feast of mercy (*Diary*, 1109). Whoever approaches the Fountain of Life on this day will be granted complete forgiveness of sins and punishment" (*Diary*, 300).

Church authorities have explained that the promise that Jesus made is not the same as a "plenary indulgence," a canonical term for the total remission of sins through the authority of the Church. In fact, the Church has not authorized a worldwide observance of the Feast of Mercy, even though it may be celebrated in parishes and at shrines with permission from the local diocese.

However, on January 23, 1995, the Sacred Congregation for Divine Worship granted to the bishops of Poland the right to establish the Sunday after Easter as the "Sunday (or Feast) of Divine Mercy" in their dioceses. And Pope John Paul II himself celebrated Divine Mercy Sunday in the diocese of Rome at the Church of the Holy Spirit on April 23, 1995.

© Marians of the Immaculate Conception

Ostra Brama, the "Dawn Gate" to the city of Vilnius. Here the image of The Divine Mercy was seen for the first time in 1935.

Chronology

August 25, 1905 — Helena Kowalska born at Glogowiec, in the District of Lodz, Poland. She's the third child of the ten children born to Stanislaus and Marianna Kowalski.

Autumn 1912 — At age seven, Helena receives "definite call of God" to religious life, though she didn't understand what religious life was.

Autumn 1914 — Helena receives her First Communion.

Autumn 1917 — Twelve-year-old Helena attends school for the first time in the district school, but is forced to leave in 1919.

Autumn 1921 — Sixteen-year-old Helena goes to work as a maid in Aleksandrow.

1922 — Helena asks for her parents' permission to enter a convent but is refused.

February, 1923 — Helena starts job as maid and babysitter for Sadowski family.

Summer 1924 — Helena has a vision of a scourged Jesus while attending a dance in Lodz. She finally decides to go to Warsaw to enter a convent.

Summer 1924 — Helena is conditionally accepted for admission to the Sisters of Our Lady of Mercy in Warsaw. She learns that she must earn the money for her wardrobe and supplies.

June 25, 1925 — Helena makes a private vow of chastity on the Feast of Corpus Christi.

August 1, 1925 — Helena enters the Sisters of Our Lady of Mercy.

April 30, 1926 — Clothing ceremony takes place, during which Helena faints after foreseeing her life of suffering. She takes the name "Sister Mary Faustina of the Most Blessed Sacrament."

Spring 1927 — A "Dark Night of the Soul" torments Sister Faustina's novitiate in Cracow.

April 20, 1928 — Sister Faustina takes First Vows in a ceremony attended by her parents.

October 31, 1928 — Transfer to Warsaw with assignment to kitchen.

February 21, 1929 — Transfer to Vilnius for temporary service as the cook.

April 1929 — Returns to Warsaw area for assignments.

May 1930 — Transfer to Plock, northwest of Warsaw.

Autumn 1930 — Illness and weakness precipitates temporary assignment to Biala, a farm owned by order.

February 22, 1931 — Apparition of Jesus of the Divine Mercy and the commission to Faustina to paint the image and have the Feast of Mercy observed.

November 1932 — Return to Warsaw to prepare for final vows.

Spring 1933 — Visit of troubled younger sister Wanda, to whom Sister Faustina ministers.

April 21, 1933 — Travels to convent at Lagiewniki near Cracow to prepare for final vows.

May 1, 1933 — Professes final vows as a Sister of Our Lady of Mercy at Lagiewniki.

May 25, 1933 — Transfer to Vilnius to serve as convent gardener.

Summer 1933 — Sister Faustina meets Father Michael Sopocko, who is to become her spiritual director. She tells him of her visions and commissions given to her by Jesus.

Autumn 1933 — At the request of Father Sopocko, Sister Faustina undergoes psychiatric tests which verify that she is a normal, balanced person.

January 2, 1934 — Accompanied by another sister, Sister Faustina visits Eugene Kazimierowski, who paints Jesus of the Divine Mercy.

Spring 1934 — Father Sopocko instructs Sister Faustina to begin a diary.

Late Spring 1934 — Acting on false inspiration, Sister Faustina burns her diary.

July 28, 1934 — Sister Faustina begins to write her diary again.

August 12, 1934 — A sudden but almost fatal illness.

January 1935 — In a vision, Sister Faustina sees the pope at Mass considering the establishment of the Feast of Mercy.

February 1935 — Sister Faustina visits her ailing mother and family in Glogowiec — a first and last visit home during religious life.

April 19, 1935 — Jesus tells Faustina on this date, Good Friday, that He wants the Divine Mercy image publicly displayed and honored in the context of a Feast of Mercy.

June 9, 1935 — Jesus tells Sister Faustina to found a new congregation dedicated to prayer for Divine Mercy.

September 13, 1935 — Faustina is given some of the prayers for the Chaplet of Divine Mercy and told to say the chaplet.

November 1935 — She composes the rule for the new contemplative congregation.

December 1935 — Sister Faustina visits the house seen in a vision, which is to be the first convent of the congregation in Vilnius.

March 1936 — She tells superiors that she plans to leave Sisters of Our Lady of Mercy in order to obey the command to found the new order. Instead, she accepts transfers to Walendow, then Derdy.

May 11, 1936 — Transferred to Cracow to be close to good medical care.

August 1936 — Receives Divine Mercy brochure being distributed by Father Sopocko.

September 1936 — Jesus tells Faustina to pray the Chaplet for Poland.

September 11, 1936 — Sister Faustina is diagnosed with advanced tuberculosis. The disease had begun to attack the intestines.

Late September 1936 — She receives invisible stigmata pains on Fridays.

December 6, 1936 — Enters tuberculosis clinic near Cracow for treatment.

March 27, 1937 — Sister Faustina is released from the clinic to return to the convent and is assigned to less tiring work as gatekeeper.

April 14, 1937 — Illness forces her to bed once again.

May 20, 1937 — Severe illness and pain returns after a respite when Faustina tells Jesus that she will endure whatever sufferings He sends.

August 27, 1937 — Father Sopocko visits Faustina in Cracow and updates her on the progress of the Divine Mercy devotions.

September 19, 1937 — Faustina's brother Stanley visits her and shares his hopes for becoming a priest.

October 10, 1937 — Faustina told by Jesus that three p.m. is the Hour of Divine Mercy. She begins to intercede in prayer especially at that hour.

April 28, 1938 — Her health again deteriorates greatly. Faustina returns to clinic.

June 1938 — Quits writing the diary due to weakness and progressing illness.

August 25, 1938 — Receives the Sacrament of the Sick at the clinic on her thirty-third birthday.

September 17, 1938 — Returns to the convent to "die at home."

October 5, 1938 — Sister Faustina dies at age thirty-three at 10:45 p.m. in her room in the convent's isolation ward.

October 7, 1938 — Funeral Mass celebrated for Faustina on the Feast of Our Lady of the Rosary. After her funeral, Sister Faustina is buried in the common cemetery at the convent at Lagiewniki near Cracow.

September 1, 1939 — Germany invades Poland and World War II begins. As Faustina had predicted, Poland suffers terribly. Pilgrims flock to her grave near Cracow. Divine Mercy devotions spread.

March 6, 1959 — The Holy See in Rome bans the Devotion to the Divine Mercy after faulty translations of Faustina's diary are misunderstood.

October, 21, 1965 — Prompted by Cardinal Karol Wojtyla of Cracow, an investigation into the life and virtues of Sister Faustina is begun.

November 25, 1966 — Sister Faustina's grave is exhumed, her remains examined and solemnly reburied inside the convent chapel at Lagiewniki.

January 31, 1968 — The process for the beatification of the Venerable

Faustina Kowalska is announced by the Congregation for the Causes of Saints.

April 15, 1978 — Following a new study of the Divine Mercy devotions requested by Cardinal Karol Wojtyla of Cracow, the Vatican ban on the devotions is lifted.

March 28, 1981 — At the tomb of Sister Faustina, Maureen Digan of Massachusetts receives a healing of lymphedema, later seen as miraculous by the Congregation for the Causes of Saints.

March 7, 1992 — Sister Faustina named "Venerable" in view of her heroic practice of Christian virtues.

April 18, 1993 — The Venerable Faustina Kowalska is beatified, becoming "Blessed Faustina Kowalska" on the Feast of Mercy in Rome.

June 7, 1997 — Pope John Paul II visits the tomb of Blessed Faustina in the Shrine of Divine Mercy at Lagiewniki, Poland. "The message of Divine Mercy has been near and dear to me," he says.

Bibliography

Barnett, Clifford R., *Poland: Its People, Its Society, Its Culture*. New Haven, Conn.: HRAF Press, 1958.

Brusher, Father Joseph S., S.J., *Popes Through the Ages*. San Rafael, Calif.: Neff-Kane, 1980.

Congregation of Marians of the Immaculate Conception, *The Promise: The Story of the Film "Divine Mercy, No Escape."* Stockbridge, Mass.: Marian Press, 1987.

Gesy, Father Lawrence J., *The Hem of His Garment: True Stories of Healing*. Huntington, Ind.: Our Sunday Visitor Publishing Division, 1996.

Grun, Bernard, *The Timetables of History: A Horizontal Linkage of People and Events*. New York: Simon and Schuster, 1975.

John Paul II, "Rich in Mercy" *(Dives in Misericordia)* in *The Pope Speaks*, Volume 26, Number 2, 1980.

Kosicki, Father George W., C.S.B., *Be Apostles of Divine Mercy*. Stockbridge, Mass.: Marian Press, 1996.

Kosicki, Father George W., C.S.B., *Special Urgency of Mercy: Why Sister Faustina?* Stockbridge, Mass.: Marian Press, 1990.

Kowalska, Mary Faustina, Blessed Sister, *Diary of Blessed Sister M. Faustina Kowalska*. Stockbridge, Mass.: Marian Press, 1987.

McAuliffe, Father Marius, O.F.M., *Pope St. Pius X: The Saint of Our Times*. New York: Catholic Book Publishing Co., 1954.

Michalenko, Father Seraphim, M.I.C. & Flynn, Vinny, *The Divine Mercy Message and Devotion*. Stockbridge, Mass.: Marian Press, 1995.

Michalenko, Sister Sophia, C.M.G.T., *Mercy My Mission: Life of Sister Faustina H. Kowalska, S.M.D.M.* Stockbridge, Mass.: Marian Press, 1987.

Sopocko, Father Michael, *God is Mercy*. St. Meinrad, Ind.: Grail Publications, 1955.

Tarnawska, Maria, *Sister Faustina Kowalska — Her Life and Mission*. Stockbridge, Mass.: Marian Press, 1989.

Welsh, David, *Adam Mickiewicz*. New York: Twayne Publishers, Inc., 1966.

Index

P

R

S

Our Sunday Visitor...
Your Source for Discovering the Riches of the Catholic Faith

Our Sunday Visitor has an extensive line of materials for young children, teens, and adults. Our books, Bibles, booklets, CD-ROMs, audios, and videos are available in bookstores worldwide.

To receive a FREE full-line catalog or for more information, call **Our Sunday Visitor** at **1-800-348-2440**. Or write, **Our Sunday Visitor /** 200 Noll Plaza / Huntington, IN 46750.

- -

Please send me: __ A catalog
Please send me materials on:
    __ Apologetics and catechetics   __ Reference works
    __ Prayer books   __ Heritage and the saints
    __ The family   __ The parish

Name_____

Address_____Apt._____

City_____State ____Zip_____

Telephone (   ) _____

                                  A73BBABP

- -

Please send a friend: __ A catalog
Please send a friend materials on:
    __ Apologetics and catechetics   __ Reference works
    __ Prayer books   __ Heritage and the saints
    __ The family   __ The parish

Name_____

Address_____Apt._____

City_____State ____Zip_____

Telephone (   ) _____

                                  A73BBABP

- -

Our Sunday Visitor
200 Noll Plaza
Huntington, IN 46750
1-800-348-2440
OSVSALES@AOL.COM

Your Source for Discovering the Riches of the Catholic Faith